# M–P
## Mexicans to Puerto Ricans

*Titles in the series*

# The NEWEST Americans

## M–P
## Mexicans to Puerto Ricans

GREENWOOD PRESS
Westport, Connecticut · London

**Library of Congress Cataloging-in-Publication Data**

Creative Media Applications
  The newest Americans.
    p. cm.–(Middle school reference)
  Includes bibliographical references and index.
  ISBN 0-313-32553-7 (set: alk. paper)–0-313-32554-5 (v.1)–0-313-32555-3 (v.2)–
  0-313-32556-1 (v.3)–0-313-32557-X (v.4)–0-313-32563-4 (v.5)
    1. Immigrants–United States–Juvenile literature–Encyclopedias.
    2. United States–Emigration and immigration–Juvenile literature–Encyclopedias.
    3. Minorities–United States–Juvenile literature–Encyclopedias.
    [1. Immigrants–United States–Encyclopedias. 2. United States–Emigration and
    immigration–Encyclopedias. 3. Minorities–Encyclopedias.] I. Series.
  JV6455.N48 2003
  304.8'73'03–dc21   2002035214

British Library Cataloguing in Publication Data is available.

Library of Congress Catalog Card Number: 2002035214
ISBN:  0–313–32553–7  (set)
        0–313–32554–5  (vol. 1)
        0–313–32555–3  (vol. 2)
        0–313–32556–1  (vol. 3)
        0–313–32557–X  (vol. 4)
        0–313–32563–4  (vol. 5)

First published in 2003

Greenwood Press, 88 Post Road West, Westport, CT 06881
An imprint of Greenwood Publishing Group, Inc.
www.greenwood.com

Printed in the United States of America

The paper used in this book complies with the Permanent Paper Standard issued by the National Information Standards Organization (Z39.48–1984).

10 9 8 7 6 5 4 3 2 1

A Creative Media Applications, Inc. Production
WRITER: Sandy Pobst
DESIGN AND PRODUCTION: Fabia Wargin Design, Inc.
EDITOR: Susan Madoff
COPYEDITOR: Laurie Lieb
PROOFREADER: Laura Walsh
ASSOCIATED PRESS PHOTO RESEARCHER: Yvette Reyes
CONSULTANT: Robert Asher, University of Connecticut

Special thanks to Donna Loughran, Christie Pfenninger, and Mary Ann Segalla for their contributions to this volume.

PHOTO CREDITS:
*Cover:* © Kim Kulish/CORBIS SABA
AP/Wide World Photographs *pages* 6, 25, 28, 31, 33, 35, 36, 39, 41, 42, 57, 58, 60, 62, 69, 71, 75, 79, 83, 91, 94, 100, 103, 107, 110, 112, 115, 117, 118, 119, 124, 126, 129, 132, 135
© Kim Kulish/CORBIS SABA *page* 14
© Bob Krist/CORBIS *page* 19
© CORBIS *page* 23
© Nik Wheeler/CORBIS *page* 45
© Bettmann/CORBIS *page* 48
© Hulton-Deuisch Collection/CORBIS *page* 51
© Lawrence Manning/CORBIS *page* 65
© Owen Franken/CORBIS *page* 85
© David Cumming; Eye Ubiquitous/CORBIS *page* 87
© Diego Lezama Orezzoli/CORBIS *page* 89
© Joseph Sohm; ChromoSohm Inc./CORBIS *page* 97
© Raymond Gehman./CORBIS *page* 108
© Jose Luis Pelaez, Inc./CORBIS *page* 121

# Contents

America
is another name
for opportunity

—*Ralph Waldo Emerson*

# A Word about
## *The Newest Americans*

This series takes a look at the people who have been coming to America from 1965 to the present. It provides historical, social, political, and cultural information on the most recent immigrant groups that are changing the face of America.

Charts and graphs show how immigration has been affected over the years, both by changes in the U.S. laws and by events in the sending country. Unless otherwise noted, the term *immigrant* in this book, including the charts and graphs, refers to new legal immigrants and to refugees and asylees who have changed their status to legal permanent residents.

From its very beginning, the United States stood for opportunity and freedom. It exists because immigrants, people who moved from their homes to make a new life in a new country, dreamed of better lives. They dreamed of having a voice in their government, of expressing their opinions and practicing their religion without fear of being imprisoned or tortured. Two hundred years later, these dreams still call to people around the world.

*opposite:*

*Puerto Rican pop star Ricky Martin won the 1999 Grammy award for Best Latin Pop Performance. His debut single "Livin' La Vida Loca" from his first English-language album became one of the biggest selling single records in U.S. music history.*

E Pluribus Unum—

# An Immigrant Nation

America declared its independence from British rule in 1776. At that time, nearly 80 percent of the people living in the colonies were white Europeans from England, Ireland, Scotland, Germany, the Netherlands, France, and Sweden. Just over 20 percent were slaves from Africa, the one group of American immigrants who did not come to this country willingly.

Over the next 200 years, more than 70 million people from around the world would *immigrate* to the United States. The majority came for *economic* reasons, eager to make the American dream a reality. Although this was one of the largest migrations of people in history, it began slowly. Wars in the United States and Europe kept immigration to a minimum until the 1820s. As things became more settled, however, a rapidly growing population that had few opportunities in Europe looked once more to America.

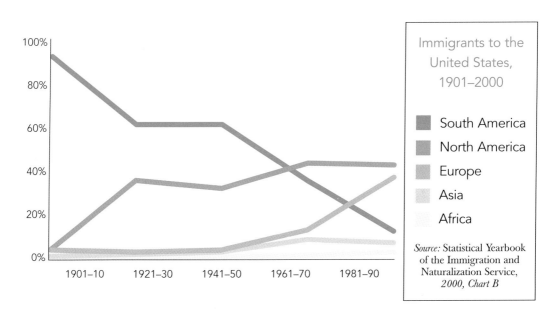

Immigrants to the United States, 1901–2000

- South America
- North America
- Europe
- Asia
- Africa

*Source:* Statistical Yearbook of the Immigration and Naturalization Service, 2000, *Chart B*

Out of Many, One

—*Motto of the United States*

## The 1800s

America offered freedom and political equality, but it also had practical attractions. Vast amounts of land unclaimed by white settlers, coupled with a growing number of jobs in the United States, exerted a strong pull on the imagination. Immigrants believed that they could improve their lives—and maybe even become wealthy—if they could only get to America.

There were many factors "pushing" immigrants to the United States as well. Population explosions, poor economic conditions, and widespread famine in Europe left many without work during the 1830s and 1840s.

The next big wave of immigrants reached American shores in the 1880s and 1890s. This time the newcomers included large numbers of southern and eastern Europeans. Immigrants from Italy, Austria-Hungary, Russia, and Poland began settling in America's cities and working in the factories.

## The 1900s

Immigration to the United States set a record in the first decade of the twentieth century. Nearly 9 million immigrants were recorded as entering the United States from 1901 to 1910.

## Immigrant Chains

Immigrant chains form when members of one immigrant family settle in America, and then convince family members and friends to join them. The established immigrants help the new immigrants find homes and work in the same area. Immigrant chains have influenced settlement patterns all over the country, helping to create large communities of Cubans in Miami, Dominicans in New York, and Chinese in San Francisco, among others.

For the first time, immigrants from southern and eastern Europe were in the majority. Many of these immigrants were Jewish and Catholic, in contrast to the predominantly Protestant groups that settled the United States. Immigration surged again from 1918 through 1921. Only when Congress enacted a quota system in 1921 and 1924 did immigration begin to decline. The *quota* system severely restricted the number of immigrants that would be allowed to enter the United States from each foreign country.

Immigration numbers remained low until the mid-1960s. But two events in particular caused America to rethink an immigration policy based on race and ethnicity. The first event was the *genocide* (systematic destruction) of European Jews during World War II. German leader Adolf Hitler's vision of a racially pure world was in direct opposition to the ideals the United States was based on. Yet the immigration policy was set up to admit primarily white Europeans. The second event was the American civil rights movement, which began in the mid-1950s and gained momentum in the 1960s. Many people felt that the United States, as a world leader, should adopt an immigration policy that would reflect its ideals of equality and freedom for everyone regardless of race or country of origin.

The Immigration and Nationality Act of 1965 introduced far-reaching changes in American immigration policy. The quota system was discarded in favor of worldwide limits. With family reunification as a priority, lawmakers allowed immediate family members of U.S. citizens to be admitted without limit.

Terrorist acts against the United States in 1993 and 2001 sparked changes to the immigration policy once again. The location of temporary (nonimmigrant) visitors, including students and businesspeople, is now being tracked more closely. The government has more freedom to investigate and detain suspected terrorists.

## Immigration Today

In 2000, nearly 850,000 people became legal immigrants. Legal immigrants, also called legal permanent residents, receive paperwork, or documentation, that shows they are living in the United States legally. The documentation, commonly called a "green card," also allows a new permanent resident to work in the United States.

American immigration laws determine how many foreigners, or aliens, can enter the United States each year. Currently, the law allows between 421,000 and 675,000 immigrants to be admitted each year. Most of the yearly admissions are reserved for family-sponsored immigrants (up to 480,000 per year). People who have job skills that are in demand, such as scientists, software programmers, and computer analysts, are also among the first chosen. They qualify for the employment-based preferences (up to 140,000 per year).

Each year, 50,000 to 55,000 immigrants enter the United States through the Diversity Program. This program addresses the inequalities of past immigration policies. Residents of countries that have sent fewer than 50,000 immigrants to the United States in each of the past five years are eligible to participate. Visas, or permits, are issued to those applicants whose names are randomly selected, giving the program its common name–the diversity lottery.

## Immigrant Admissions in 2000

| | | |
|---|---|---|
| a | Immediate relative of U.S. citizen | 41% |
| b | Family preference | 28% |
| c | Employment preference | 13% |
| d | Refugee/asylee adjustment | 8% |
| e | Diversity Program | 6% |
| f | Other | 4% |

*Source: Immigration and Naturalization Service*

# Immigration Legislation

Until the late 1800s, there were few federal restrictions on immigration. States had the ability to control or limit immigration. This changed in 1875 when the federal government gained control of immigration. Beginning in the 1920s, the laws also specified the number of immigrants that could come to the United States each year.

Here is a brief description of the laws that have changed American immigration patterns over the past 200 years:

1882    The *Chinese Exclusion Act* stopped nearly all new immigration from China. Chinese immigrants would not be admitted in large numbers again until the 1950s.

1907    The so-called *Gentlemen's Agreement* blocked most Japanese immigration. A presidential order kept Hawaiian Japanese from moving to the United States.

1917    The *1917 Immigration Act* required immigrants to pass a literacy test before entering the United States. It also created a zone covering most of Asia. No immigration from this zone was allowed.

1921     The *Quota Act* temporarily limited immigration after World War I. Immigration limits were based on national origin. Immigrants from the Western Hemisphere were not subject to limits.

1924     The *1924 Immigration Act* established the first permanent limits on immigration, continuing the national origins quota system. Before this law was enacted, the idea of illegal immigration did not exist.

1952     The *Immigration and Nationality Act of 1952* lifted some of the restrictions on Asian countries. Discrimination based on gender was eliminated. For the first time, preference was given to foreigners whose skills were in demand and to relatives of U.S. citizens and residents. Race-based limits were abolished when all races became eligible for naturalization.

1965     The groundbreaking *Immigration and Nationality Act of 1965* (also known as the Hart-Cellar Act) eliminated the quota system for worldwide limits.

1980     The *Refugee Act of 1980* established procedures for admitting and resettling *refugees*. It also made a distinction between refugees and asylees.

1986     The *Immigration Reform and Control Act (IRCA)* attempted to address the problem of illegal immigration. It provided an opportunity for immigrants who were living and working illegally in the United States before January 1, 1982, to adjust their status and eventually become legal residents and naturalized citizens.

1990     The *Immigration Act of 1990* made several major changes in U.S. policy. The total number of immigrants and refugees allowed to enter the United States each year increased dramatically. A Diversity Program allowed immigrants from countries that were underrepresented in America in the past an extra chance to receive a visa.

1996     The *Antiterrorism and Effective Death Penalty Act* outlined measures to identify and remove terrorists from the United States. It allowed the U.S. government to use evidence collected in secret to accuse immigrants of terrorist acts.

1996    The *Welfare Reform Act* was designed to keep most legal immigrants from getting food stamps and supplemental security income provided by the federal government.

1996    The *Illegal Immigration Reform and Immigrant Responsibility Act* focused on improving control of the U.S. borders.

2001    The *U.S.A. Patriot Act* expanded the government's ability to investigate, arrest, and deport legal residents for failing to comply with immigration regulations. Immigrants (including legal residents) who were suspected of terrorism could now be held indefinitely in detention centers.

## Refugees and Asylees

Some people have to leave their countries because it isn't safe to live there anymore. Those who are afraid to return to their country because of persecution ask countries like the United States to take them in. People who are living outside the United States when they apply for protection are called refugees. They often have to wait years before their application is granted. The number of refugees permitted to resettle in the United States each year is determined by the president after discussions with Congress.

Like refugees, asylees are also seeking *asylum*, or safety from persecution. The difference is that asylees make their way to the United States before they ask for asylum. Most asylees come from countries that are located near the United States, such as Cuba, Nicaragua, and Guatemala.

## Illegal Immigrants

In addition to the nearly 1 million legal immigrants who arrive in the United States each year, hundreds of thousands of people enter the country without permission. No one really knows how many illegal immigrants enter the United States each year. The Immigration and Naturalization Service (INS) estimates the number at close to 300,000 per year. These immigrants don't have the papers (visas) that show they have been admitted legally to the United States. They are often referred to as undocumented aliens or illegal immigrants.

In 1996, the INS estimated that 5 million undocumented immigrants were living in the United States. Today, experts suggest that the number is between 6 and 9 million. Over half are from Mexico. Because it is easier for people from nearby countries to enter the United States illegally, eight of the top ten countries sending illegal immigrants are in Central America, the Caribbean, and North America. The other two are the Philippines and Poland.

*A group of new Americans takes the oath of citizenship at the Los Angeles convention center.*

# Becoming Naturalized Citizens

American citizens enjoy many rights that permanent residents and visitors do not have. American citizens have the right to vote to select their leaders. They may hold government jobs and run for elected office. They can ask the government to allow family members to come to live in the United States. American citizens can also apply for a U.S. passport, making it easier to travel abroad.

Anyone who is born in the United States is automatically a citizen. Immigrants who want to become citizens must go through a process called naturalization. Before permanent residents can become naturalized citizens, they must live in the United States for a specified amount of time, usually three to five years. Once the residency requirement has been met, the resident must submit an application to the INS. A criminal check is completed during the application process.

The next step is an interview between the applicant and an INS officer. The ability to speak English is judged throughout the interview. Questions about the history and government of the United States test the immigrant's understanding of American civics. At the end of the interview, the officer either approves or denies the application for citizenship. An applicant who fails one of the tests may be given a second chance to pass the test.

Applicants who successfully complete the naturalization process attend a naturalization ceremony at which they swear an oath of allegiance to the United States. Each new citizen then receives a Certificate of Naturalization. Children under eighteen automatically become citizens when their parents take the oath of allegiance.

## American Attitudes toward Immigration

Throughout America's history, immigrants have been both welcomed and feared. Negative attitudes toward immigrants tend to increase when the economy is in a slump. Increased competition for jobs and fears for the future lead many Americans to close ranks.

## Discrimination

From the start, immigrants faced *discrimination* in America regardless of their race. Irish-Catholic, Japanese, Chinese, and Filipino immigrants have all been targets of hostility through the years.

Immigrants today continue to struggle to fit in. They are judged by their ability to speak English, their skin color, their clothing. Immigrant children comment that their new English vocabulary includes words like "discrimination," "prejudice," and "stereotype."

# Immigration Myths and Realities

The debate over immigration has been heated from time to time. Amazingly, the same arguments against immigration have been made for over 100 years. Below are some of the claims that are often made about immigrants. The facts are also given.

| *Myth* | *Reality* |
| --- | --- |
| Immigrants take jobs away from Americans. | New immigrants usually accept low-paying jobs that Americans don't want or won't accept. Immigrants often revitalize urban areas. Many open new businesses, providing jobs for others. |
| There are too many immigrants today. They outnumber Americans. | The actual number of immigrants in recent years does exceed that of past years. Immigrants in the 1990s, however, made up less than 3 percent of the population, compared to 9.6 percent from 1901 to 1910. |
| Immigrants come to America because they want to receive financial assistance, called welfare, from the government. | New immigrants must prove that they won't be a burden before they are allowed to enter the United States. Historically, new immigrants are more likely to be employed, save more of their earnings, and are more likely to start new businesses than native-born Americans. Recently, however, the percentage of immigrants receiving welfare is nearing that of native-born Americans. |
| Immigrants keep to themselves and speak their own languages. They don't want to be Americans. | Immigrants know that English is the key to success in the United States. Classes teaching English as a second language fill up quickly. There is usually a waiting list. Studies show that children of immigrants actually prefer English. |
| There is too much diversity among immigrants today. *Ethnic* enclaves, or communities, mean that immigrants don't have to adapt to the U.S. *culture*. | Some social scientists argue that *ethnic* enclaves form when immigration is not diverse enough. |

# The Immigrant Experience

## Destinations

Along immigrants to the United States have to make life-altering decisions that will change the course of their future. Their decisions are usually based on three main factors: location of family members, if any; opportunities for work; and proximity, or closeness, to their home country. These three factors have influenced settlement patterns since immigrants first began arriving on America's shores.

Although immigrants can live anywhere in the United States, nearly two-thirds of them settle in just six states. California, New York, Florida, Texas, New Jersey, and Illinois count more immigrants among their population than all other states combined. California alone is the destination of one-fourth of the nation's immigrants.

Because finding work and living near others who share their experience is so important, nearly all new immigrants (93 percent) live in urban areas. The most popular U.S. destinations in 2000 were New York City, Los Angeles, Miami, Chicago, and Washington, D.C.

Refugees do not necessarily follow these same settlement patterns, at least when they first arrive. As part of their relocation package, they are resettled into communities across the United States. Individuals or families in that community *sponsor* the refugees, helping them get used to their new surroundings. When refugees adjust their status to immigrant, they often choose to move to a location with a larger immigrant community.

| Immigrant Destinations | |
|---|---|
| *a* California | 25.6% |
| *b* New York | 12.5% |
| *c* Florida | 11.6% |
| *d* Texas | 7.5% |
| *e* New Jersey | 4.7% |
| *f* Illinois | 4.3% |
| *g* All other states | 33.8% |

*Source: Immigration and Naturalization Service*

# Fitting In

Social scientists call the process of adapting to a new culture *assimilation*. Assimilation takes place over time and in different ways. There is economic assimilation, in which immigrants take advantage of workplace opportunities to increase their income. Social and cultural assimilation take place as immigrants form friendships with Americans at school and at work. English skills improve and cultural traditions from their home country may be adapted. Young people especially become immersed in the American culture and begin to adopt those values. Finally, there is political assimilation. This occurs when immigrants choose to complete the naturalization process so their voices can be heard in their government.

# CHAPTER ONE

# Mexicans

# Mexico,

America's neighbor to the south, shares a history as well as a border with the United States. Few other nations have had as much influence on the growth and development of the United States as Mexico. Much of the western United States was once part of Mexico. About 20 million U.S. citizens and residents proudly claim Mexican heritage, both as recent *immigrants* and as families who have lived in the United States for over a century.

Mexico was once a Spanish *colony* and 60 percent of its people are mestizo. Mestizos have both Spanish and Amerindian ancestors. About 30 percent of Mexicans are Amerindian, *descendants* of the Aztecs, Mayas, or other indigenous people. Whites make up only 9 percent of Mexico's population, while about 1 percent of Mexicans belong to an *ethnic group* other than those listed here.

## A Quick Look Back

The earliest known *civilization* in Mexico was developed by the Olmecs, who established colonies in central and southern Mexico. Many stone sculptures have been found from this period.

The Mayan *culture,* which was at its peak between A.D. 200 and 800, is one of the best-known cultures of Mexico. The Maya developed a system of writing that they used to record astronomy, history, and religion. Their system of mathematics was very advanced and not equaled for centuries in Europe.

Nobody really knows why the Mayan culture declined, but some scientists think that the Mayans were attacked by neighboring tribes or hurt by natural disasters.

The Aztecs emerged as the most powerful of the Mexican Indian tribes in the fourteenth century. They built complex cities and temples. Their belief in human sacrifice made them feared by other Amerindian groups, who helped the Spanish conquerors overthrow the Aztecs early in the sixteenth century.

## Spanish Conquest

The Spanish conquerors, led by Hernán Cortés, arrived in Mexico in 1519. Within two years, the Spanish defeated the Aztecs. They tore down the Aztec capital and built the city that would later be known as Mexico City. As in other Latin American countries, the Roman Catholic Church introduced Spanish culture to the region. Priests established schools and hospitals in the cities and missions in the rural areas. They worked to convert native people to Christianity. Many Amerindians died soon after Spain's conquest, either by diseases such as measles and smallpox or through overwork as forced labor.

### Did you know?

According to legend, early Aztecs settled near present-day Mexico City because they saw a vision of an island in the middle of a lake. On the island, an eagle holding a serpent in its mouth perched on a cactus. This vision was taken as a sign from the gods to settle there. Today, the eagle with a serpent in its mouth is the state symbol of Mexico and appears on the Mexican flag.

## Mexican Independence

By the beginning of the nineteenth century, Spain's control over Mexico was fading. In 1810, Father Miguel Hidalgo y Costilla signaled the beginning of the fight for freedom from Spain with his Grito de Dolores (GREE-toh day-doh-LOR-ays), a call for independence made from his church pulpit in the Mexican town of Dolores. Amerindians joined with mestizos to fight for an independent Mexico. Hidalgo was later executed for treason, but the fight for independence continued.

After eleven years of fighting, Mexico won its independence from Spain. The Roman Catholic Church was established as the official church of the new country. Although Mexico was initially set up as a monarchy, it became a republic one year later, in 1823. The southern region of the former colony—present-day Guatemala, El Salvador, Honduras, Nicaragua, and Costa Rica—broke away to become the United Provinces of Central America.

## The New Republic

The people of Mexico faced a daunting task in rebuilding their new nation. Years of fighting had destroyed much of Mexico's *economy,* as well as the trust between its people. Two distinct factions emerged as the new nation struggled to create a strong government. The conservative group included those who were already wealthy or powerful, such as church leaders, landowners, and members of the military. They wanted life in Mexico to stay much the way it had been in the past, with a powerful few governing the country and the Catholic Church in control of education. The liberals, on the other hand, sought to limit the powers of the church. They wanted to establish a system of public education and social reforms that would be funded by the government instead of the church. And they wanted to form a government that shared power with the individual states. Although the conservatives and liberals had completely different goals and views of how government should operate, both groups were dominated by the *peninsulares* and *criollos,* people of European ancestry. These two groups continue to dominate Mexican politics today.

## Changing Borders

In 1820, the Mexican government agreed to allow immigrants from the United States into northern Mexico (present-day Texas). The Americans soon outnumbered the Mexicans who had settled in the region. By 1835, Texans were demanding their independence, angry about changes in the Mexican *constitution* that banned continued American immigration to Texas, outlawed slavery, and limited the Mexican states' autonomy. In 1836, Texans defeated General Antonio López de Santa Anna's troops and declared Texas an independent republic. Mexico never officially recognized Texas's new status, however. The new republic claimed the Rio Grande as its western and southern boundary, making it much larger than the original Mexican state of Tejas. The Mexican government considered the Nueces River to be the boundary of Texas. These different opinions about the boundary line contributed to the Mexican-American War (1846–1848) a decade later.

*Mexican general and dictator Antonio Lopez de Santa Anna is shown on horseback in this drawing from 1852.*

In 1845, U.S. president James Polk offered to purchase present-day California and New Mexico from Mexico, hoping to expand the number of slave states and please the Southern Democrats who supported him. The Mexican government refused the offer. When Texas joined the United States in December 1845, the Mexican government ended its diplomatic relationship with the United States.

In 1846, Polk sent General Zachary Taylor and his troops to the Rio Grande, ordering them to enforce the boundary claimed by Texas. Mexico, believing that the Rio Grande lay fully within its territory, responded by ordering Mexican troops to cross the river to meet Taylor's army. The U.S. Congress then declared war on Mexico, launching the Mexican-American War.

When the war ended two years later, the United States possessed the region that includes California, Nevada, Utah, and parts of Wyoming, Colorado, New Mexico, and Arizona. Later, the United States purchased a strip of land from Mexico that became southern Arizona and New Mexico. Known as the Gadsden Purchase, it formed the final border between the United States and Mexico.

## La Reforma

The conservatives and liberals continued to fight for power after the Mexican-American War. Three years of war between the conservatives and liberals followed, with the liberals finally gaining control of the country. In 1861, Benito Juárez was elected president.

Later that year, the French emperor Napoleon III sent French troops to Mexico. The stated purpose was to collect payments for debts incurred during the Mexican-American War. But the troops were instructed to take control of Mexico City and make Napoleon's relative, Archduke Maximilian of Austria, ruler of Mexico.

When the American Civil War ended in 1865, the United States sent weapons and ammunition to Mexico to help in its fight against the French invaders. The United States also encouraged American soldiers to join the Mexican army in the fight against the French. In 1867, the French were finally driven from Mexico. Juárez returned to Mexico City and called for presidential elections, which he won. He served as president until his death in 1872 and is remembered as one of Mexico's greatest leaders.

## A Dictatorship Emerges

Upon Juárez's death in 1872, Sebastián Lerdo de Tejada (say-bah-stee-AHN LAIR-doh day-tay-HAH-dah), the head of Mexico's supreme court, became president. When Lerdo wanted to run for reelection in 1876—an action that was unconstitutional, Porfirio Díaz (por-FEAR-ee-oh DEE-ahz) led a successful revolt. Lerdo fled the country to live in *exile* in the United States and Díaz took control of Mexico City, naming himself president.

Díaz was well respected when he first took office, but his popularity plunged as he established a *dictatorship* to rule the country. He took land belonging to the Amerindians and gave it to wealthy landowners who grew products to sell to other countries. The poor no longer had enough land to grow their own food and could not earn enough to purchase the food that was imported, or brought in, from other countries. Education and other social programs were neglected. The cry for change grew louder.

Díaz finally agreed to hold an election in 1910, but fixed it so that he won. Francisco Madero (fran-SIS-koh mah-DAIR-oh), the liberal candidate for president, was imprisoned by Díaz just before the election. When released, Madero fled to the United States, where he lived in exile.

## The Mexican Revolution

On November 20, 1910, a call by Madero for Mexican citizens to take up arms against the government marked the start of the Mexican Revolution (1910–1920). Madero returned to Mexico and joined forces with revolutionary leaders Emiliano Zapata (eh-*meel*-ee-AH-no sah-PAH-tah) and Pancho Villa (PON-choh VEE-yah). They succeeded in evicting Díaz from office in 1911.

Zapata led revolts in the south, demanding that land be given back to the native people, while Villa led revolts in northern Mexico.

Under the leadership of Venustiano Carranza, a new constitution was written in 1917. Land was to be returned to the native people, the power of the Catholic Church was limited, and presidents could serve only one term. The new constitution also provided for labor unions to protect workers and national ownership of petroleum, silver, and other mineral resources. Because Carranza didn't support the more radical reforms, he ignored them and the revolution continued.

In 1928, Plutarco Elías Calles (ploo-TAR-koh ay-LEE-ahs KAH-yays) created the National Revolutionary Party (Spanish acronym PNR), a political party that still exists today as the Institutional Revolutionary Party (Spanish acronym PRI). Calles's intent in creating the party was to run the country through "puppet presidents"—presidents who would follow his (and later, the party leaders') directions. The party grew so powerful that its nominee was elected president in every election from 1928 until 2000.

Calles effectively controlled Mexican politics until 1934, when his selected candidate—Lázaro Cárdenas—was elected president. Cárdenas ignored Calles's directives and began a series of radical reforms that outraged the conservatives. Land was seized from wealthy landowners and restored as communal farms for the native Indians. The railway system and petroleum industry were nationalized. When Calles objected to these reforms, Cárdenas sent him into exile.

The election in 1940 of Manuel Ávila Camacho marked the end of revolutionary changes in Mexico. Conservatives were appeased when some of the land reform policies instituted under Cárdenas were reversed.

*Emiliano Zapata is widely renowned as the voice of the Mexican revolution, which began in 1910 because peasants were angry with the government for stealing their land.*

# After the Revolution

During World War II (1939–1945), Mexico sided with the Allied forces. About 250,000 Mexican nationals served in the U.S. military. Thousands more became braceros (brah-SAIR-ohs), temporary hired hands who worked in America's factories and fields, replacing the American workers who were fighting overseas.

After the war, Miguel Alemán Valdés became the first civilian president since the beginning of the revolution. For the first time, a president staffed the government with more college graduates than military officers. Emphasis was placed on industrial and agricultural growth. During his term (1946–1952), the middle class grew, but the poor didn't make much progress.

The 1950s and 1960s were years of increasing unrest. Discontent with rampant corruption and vast disparities in income and opportunities between upper and lower classes resulted in protests and demonstrations. Police and military troops were often brought in to end the protests.

# Growing Problems

Rapid population growth and a decline in the economy led to high unemployment rates in the 1970s. Millions of people from rural areas moved to the cities in search of work. Housing wasn't readily available, and slums grew up around most cities. Malnutrition was a major problem, with an estimated half of the population not able to afford the food they needed to survive. The government increased wages and distributed land to the poor, but these programs met with limited success. Higher wages and better living conditions drew many Mexicans to the United States.

Things looked brighter in the mid-1970s when major oil reserves were discovered and developed in Mexico. Oil prices were high and the money from the oil was used to develop an industrial base for the country. (Countries that manufacture and sell goods often have a more stable and profitable economy than those that rely on a single resource, such as oil or agricultural exports.) The government borrowed millions of dollars from foreign banks against future oil earnings to pay for the construction.

Unfortunately, worldwide oil prices dropped dramatically in the early 1980s, leaving Mexico with a massive debt and no way to repay it. A loan from the International Monetary Fund

(IMF) helped the country stay afloat, but the government had to raise taxes to pay off the loan, an action that was not popular with most Mexicans.

Although the PRI continued to dominate Mexican politics, the people were growing increasingly frustrated with the inability of the government to address the country's problems, which by the 1980s included government corruption linked to drug trafficking, a decline in the standard of living for most Mexicans, and huge foreign debt.

In 1988, Carlos Salinas de Gortari, despite strong opposition to his presidency, revitalized Mexico's economy by encouraging foreign investment, increasing exports, and selling several state-owned companies. His most important contributions were to negotiate a free-trade agreement in Central America as well as the North American Free Trade Agreement between Mexico, the United States, and Canada. Although the changes were good for the country, once again, Mexico's poorest citizens did not see any improvement in their daily life.

## The 1990s

In the 1990s, once again, the United States and the IMF loaned Mexico $50.5 billion to stabilize the economy. Mexico had to agree to implement financial reforms recommended by the IMF, including raising the price of gasoline and electricity and cutting government spending. Mexico was thus able to repay the U.S. portion of the loan in three years. Today, Mexico's economy continues to grow, although slowly.

## The International Monetary Fund

The International Monetary Fund (IMF) was established by the Allies after World War II to stabilize the international economy. Member countries agree to pay a quota, or fee, to join the IMF. This fee is based on a country's economic position in relation to other members. The amount of the quota determines the voting power of each country as well as its eligibility to obtain financing. The United States is the largest of the 184 members of the IMF.

One of the most visible roles of the IMF is lending money to countries that are experiencing financial crises or recovering from natural disasters or war. In return for a loan, a country must agree to implement the economic policies recommended by the IMF. These policies are designed to help the country develop long-term economic growth and pay back the loan.

*President Vicente Fox speaks during a news conference at his official residence, Los Pinos, in Mexico City.*

# Mexico Today

In 2000, the National Action Party (Spanish acronym PAN) candidate, Vicente Fox, was elected president. He became the first person from an opposition party to win a presidential election since the PRI was founded in 1928. He inherited a government in which corruption is widespread. Over half of the population lives in poverty. Most of Mexico's wealth is concentrated in the hands of an elite few. Without any government-sponsored assistance programs, many children have to leave school and work to help their family earn a living. As many as 5 million children under the age of twelve work rather than attend school. The rampant poverty in Mexico is also what drives many people to *immigrate* to the United States.

Fox's immediate goals upon election were to reorganize the government, reduce poverty, and reorganize the armed forces and police. He and U.S. president George W. Bush also pledged to create a plan that addressed immigration and work issues for the two countries. Before the negotiations could begin, however, a series of *terrorist* attacks on American soil claimed the attention of the United States. The U.S.-Mexico immigration initiative remains a low priority for the United States at this time.

# North American Free Trade Agreement

In 1992, Mexico, the United States, and Canada signed the North American Free Trade Agreement (NAFTA). One of the most important aspects of NAFTA is that it eliminated the tariffs on all goods traded between the countries. (Tariffs are taxes charged on goods that are shipped into or out of a country. They make the product more expensive for the consumer to buy.) The agreement was controversial in America because workers feared that corporations would move their manufacturing operations to Mexico, where the cost of labor is much lower.

Experts predict that one long-term effect of NAFTA will be to reduce illegal immigration into the United States. With well-paying jobs available in Mexico, its citizens would not need to travel to the United States in search of work.

| Mexican Population in the U.S. | |
|---|---|
| California | 8,716,179 |
| Texas | 5,693,173 |
| Arizona | 1,119,523 |
| Illinois | 1,116,598 |
| *Source: U.S. Census, 2000* | |

# Coming to America

The earliest Mexican Americans didn't have to leave their homes or families to come to the United States. Instead, the United States came to them. When Texas became a state in 1845 and after the United States won control over California and the Southwest, tens of thousands of Mexicans were given the choice of staying and becoming American citizens or moving to Mexico. Nearly all decided to stay.

A growing need for agricultural workers in the United States drew immigrants from Mexico from 1900 to 1930. When the United States entered World War I (1914–1918) in 1917, many agricultural producers and factories were left shorthanded. A factor in the jump in immigration from Mexico during this period was the *quota system* passed by the U.S. Congress in 1924 that

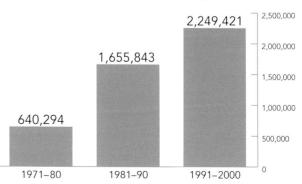

U.S./Mexican Immigration by Decade

1971–80: 640,294
1981–90: 1,655,843
1991–2000: 2,249,421

*Source:* Statistical Yearbook of the Immigration and Naturalization Service

strictly limited immigration from eastern Europe. From the first decade of the 1900s to the third, the number of Mexican immigrants increased nearly 1,000 percent. Most of these immigrants settled in California, Texas, and the southwestern states, although some worked in factories in the Midwest.

Concern over the growing numbers of immigrants led to the creation of the U.S. Border Patrol in 1924. Its responsibility was the enforcement of Immigration and Naturalization Service (INS) policies, especially stopping illegal immigration.

## Changing Policies

The stock market crash of 1929 and the Great Depression of the early 1930s meant hard times for everyone. Many Americans lost their jobs and had trouble supporting their families. Immigrants from all countries faced the same hardships as native-born Americans. But they also received much of the blame for the problem; many Americans felt that immigrants were taking the few available jobs away from American citizens.

Mexican immigrants, because of their country's proximity to the United States, were targeted by two special programs. First, there was a concentrated effort to deport those Mexicans who had entered the United States illegally. Unfortunately, because of the racist attitudes of that time, many American citizens of Mexican descent were included in the group of Mexicans who were sent back to Mexico. Second, the U.S. government encouraged Mexicans who were residing in America legally to return to Mexico by offering free transportation and other incentives.

In 1940, the momentum changed again. When the United States declared war on Japan and entered World War II in 1941, the departure of thousands of soldiers left factories and farms shorthanded. Once again, the United States turned to its southern neighbor for help.

## The Bracero Program

By 1942, the United States and Mexico had negotiated an agreement allowing Mexicans to cross the border to work in the fields on a temporary basis. At the end of the season, these braceros or hired hands, would return to Mexico. While in America, the workers were to be given housing, food, and medical care in addition to their pay. The program was poorly enforced and many of the braceros found themselves living in grim, crowded conditions in unheated shacks. Still, drawn by opportunities that simply weren't available in Mexico, over 4 million workers participated in the Bracero Program between 1942 and 1964.

The Bracero Program was cut back in the mid-1940s as American servicemen returned to work after World War II, although it was rekindled in 1951. Many employers continued to recruit and hire Mexican workers, even those without documentation, and paid them less than the U.S. minimum wage. Obtaining the legal documents necessary for entering the United States legally was time-consuming and expensive, even though there were no numerical limits on immigration from Mexico. Since the Border Patrol couldn't police the entire border, many Mexicans simply walked or swam across the border to work in the fields and ranches from Texas to California.

*Braceros pick cucumbers in Michigan in 1963. The word bracero means "day-laborer" or "strong-armed man" in Spanish.*

## Braceros

According to the agreement between Mexico and the United States, 10 percent of the braceros' already low pay was automatically deducted and placed in a savings account. This money was to be given to the braceros when they returned to Mexico. Most workers, however, never received the money. Some never even knew it was being deducted from their pay, since all contracts were in English. But even those who knew about the program and tried to withdraw their savings ran into trouble. Requirements such as having to travel to Mexico City to file the paperwork made it virtually impossible for most braceros to collect their money.

From 1949 to 1953, the number of illegal immigrants captured by the Border Patrol increased from nearly 300,000 to 865,000. In an effort to stop the flow of illegal immigrants, U.S. laws against illegal immigration were strengthened. By 1959, nearly 4 million immigrants had been deported, including some children–American citizens by birth–who were sent to Mexico with their parents.

About 300,000 Mexican Americans served in the military during World War II. When they returned home to America, many used their military benefits to further their education and purchase homes. Having experienced racial equality in the military, they also began to demand equal treatment in their daily lives in America. Organizations such as the League of United Latin American Citizens and the Mexican American Legal Defense and Education Fund helped Mexican Americans to fight segregation, seek educational opportunities, and gain equal protection under the law.

## The Illegal Immigration Issue

Since the 1960s, Mexico has been the largest source of immigrants to the United States, both legal and illegal. It is the illegal immigration that has caught the attention of most Americans, however. Anywhere from 1 to 3 million people—most of them Mexican—are estimated to cross the U.S. border illegally each year, a number that includes those who cross the border multiple times.

Most of those who enter the United States without proper documentation are looking for work. Although employers are supposed to make sure that they hire only documented workers, many don't. They are able to pay illegal immigrants less than the minimum wage, often threatening to turn workers over to the Immigration and Naturalization Service (INS) for deportation if they complain.

## New Laws, New Complaints

The 1965 Immigration and Nationality Act offered more Mexicans the ability to become legal residents of the United States. In addition, Mexican Americans and legal residents could now sponsor family members. From the 1950s to the 1960s, legal immigration from Mexico nearly doubled. Illegal immigration continued, too, as people who could not make a living in Mexico crossed the border in search of work.

As the U.S. economy soured in the 1980s, complaints about illegal immigration increased. The U.S. Congress passed a law in 1986 called the Immigration Reform and Control Act (IRCA). This law stated that people who could prove that they were living and working in the United States as of January 1, 1982, were eligible for amnesty. That is, instead of being deported for being in the country illegally, they would be allowed to become legal residents. Once they were legal residents, they could apply to become naturalized citizens. Thousands of illegal immigrants, the majority of whom were Mexican, took advantage of this program. Their numbers are reflected in the immigration statistics: The 1980s brought 1 million more Mexicans to America than came in the 1970s.

Immigration from Mexico peaked in 1991 when nearly 1 million immigrants were recorded. Not all of these immigrants were newly arrived; many were adjusting their status to legal permanent resident as a result of the IRCA law. Immigration from Mexico averaged 150,000 a year from 1996 to 2000. Most of today's immigrants enter through the family reunification program. Even though the number of immigrants is leveling off, Mexico still sends more immigrants to America than any other country. In the 1990s, Mexico sent almost as many immigrants as all of the countries in Asia.

*Lee Treviño kisses the British Open Golf Championship cup after he won the title for the second year in a row in Muirfield, Scotland, in July 1972.*

The most recent Mexican immigrants aren't stopping in border states like Texas and California, as in the past. Instead, many are settling in regions that aren't traditional destinations, such as North Carolina, Wisconsin, and New York City.

## *Spotlight on*
### LEE TREVIÑO

Lee Treviño didn't fit the profile of a professional golfer back in 1968. For one thing, he had dropped out of school in the seventh grade and worked as a caddy at a golf course, where he taught himself how to play golf. For another, he was Mexican American, a rarity on the golf course in those days.

Born in Dallas, Texas, in 1939, Lee Treviño proved to everyone that he deserved to be a professional golfer when, two years after turning pro, he won the prestigious U.S. Open in 1968. In 1971, he won three major tournaments within twenty days: the U.S. Open, the Canadian Open, and the British Open. The same year he was named Player of the Year by the Professional Golfer's Association (PGA) and Athlete of the Year by *Sports Illustrated* and the Associated Press.

In 1975, Treviño was playing in a Chicago tournament when he was struck by lightning. Although he was able to continue playing golf, the incident caused ongoing back problems.

Treviño won the PGA Championship in 1974 and again in 1984. He was inducted into the World Golf Hall of Fame in 1981. After retiring from the regular PGA circuit in 1985 with twenty-seven wins, he began playing on the U.S. Senior Tour in 1990. Treviño has continued his winning style on the Senior Tour, racking up 29 wins.

# Life in America

## Family

Latino families are generally very close, and Mexicans are no different. Unlike immigrant families who are separated for years before they are reunited in America, Mexican families tend to immigrate together. If one or both parents do enter the United States before their children, the period of separation is likely to be short—a matter of months rather than years in most cases.

In America as in Mexico, several generations of a family may share a home. Traditionally, the oldest man is the head of the family, and the father is an authority figure. Women have an honored role as mother, but don't have much input in traditional homes. However, parents of Mexican American families in the middle and upper classes often share the responsibilities of supporting their families at work and at home.

One of the biggest differences between Mexican families and American families is in each family's expectations for their children. As Mexican children grow older, they are expected to help take care of their family. Middle children may assume responsibility for watching younger brothers and sisters, while older children often work to help support the family. The needs of the family take priority over any one individual family member's desires. This commitment is evident when the oldest children in a family give up their opportunities for further education and work so that their younger siblings can attend college.

American values are nearly the opposite. Young people are encouraged to grow away from their parents and families and become more independent. They take part in activities that they find interesting or that will further their education.

## Work

Mexicans and Mexican Americans work in every conceivable job in the United States. They are chief executive officers of corporations and farmworkers, bank presidents and housekeepers, astronauts, factory workers, computer programmers, construction workers, and teachers. However, the most visible roles for the hundreds of thousands of new immigrants entering the United States each year from Mexico are as low-paid, unskilled laborers, working in agriculture and service industries. This, coupled with the fact that most illegal immigrants are from Mexico, has led to widespread, ongoing *discrimination* against Mexicans and Mexican Americans.

## Following the Crops

Many Mexican and Mexican Americans are migrant workers. Migrant workers follow the crops, planting and harvesting crops in one region, then moving on to the next. It is backbreaking work with long hours and little pay, but for many who have little education and speak little English, migrant farming represents an opportunity to earn money for their families.

Not only are the working and living conditions miserable, but migrant workers often have to deal with unscrupulous employers. The owner of the fields may spray pesticides, or poison that kills insects, on the crops while workers are in the field, causing serious health problems for the workers. Sometimes the paychecks aren't valid; that is, the employer doesn't have enough money in the bank to pay the workers. Other employers wait until the workers complete the job, then report them to the INS as illegal immigrants. (An estimated 20 to 50 percent of farmworkers are in the United States illegally.)

# *Spotlight on*
## CÉSAR CHÁVEZ

*César Chávez gestures as he speaks during a news conference in Los Angeles in 1989. Chávez, president of the United Farm Workers, said during the news conference that the union's boycott of California table grapes was a success.*

César Chávez was only ten years old when his family moved to California. The family had lost their land near Yuma, Arizona, where Chávez was born, in the aftermath of the 1930s Depression. After completing eighth grade, Chávez started working in the fields with his family, planting row after row of vegetables and picking box after box of fruit.

In 1952, Chávez began working for the Community Service Organization (CSO), a California-based group that helped Mexican Americans become registered voters and fought against discrimination. He pushed for the CSO to create a labor union for farmworkers. When his efforts were unsuccessful, Chávez quit his position with the CSO in order to work directly with the farmworkers to organize the National Farm Workers Association. This union merged with the United Farm Workers in 1966.

César Chávez led strikes to protest poor working conditions. He also organized boycotts of agricultural products. (In a boycott, people agree not to buy certain goods until the producers make certain changes, such as providing rest periods and clean water for the workers to drink or paying higher wages.) Chávez also fasted, or went for long periods of time without food, to publicize conditions that farmworkers had to endure. In 1988, he fasted for thirty-six days to protest the use of pesticides that poison migrant workers, including the children who work in the fields.

In 1994, U.S. president Bill Clinton awarded Chávez the Presidential Medal of Freedom, the nation's highest civilian honor. In California, Arizona, and Texas, César Chávez's birthday—March 31—is observed by a state holiday.

# School

Mexican American students, even when they are in a predominantly Hispanic school, feel the effects of prejudice. Some believe that they are automatically placed in lower-level classes because they are from Mexico. Others struggle to do well in an environment in which they know neither English or Spanish, but rather an indigenous language such as Nahuatl. They speak of the frustration they feel when they know the answer to a question but can't express it in English.

Many Mexican children arrive in the United States eager to further their education. Those whose families settle in predominantly low-income urban areas, however, may face additional obstacles before reaching their goals. Often the most surprising problem is the harassment they receive from Mexican American students who have given up on the educational system. They make fun of newcomers who want to study and excel, accusing them of trying to be "white." New students endure teasing and name-calling, a situation which seems to be universal for immigrant children.

Children of migrant farmworkers have special challenges in completing their education. Because their families move so often, they attend several schools during the course of the school year. Sometimes they are kept out of school to watch younger siblings or to work in the fields with their family. In years past, each school would have to assess the students' abilities to determine where to place them. School records often didn't arrive at the new school until the student was gone. Because they missed school so often, many students gave up and dropped out.

A special program is now in place to help migrant children stay in school. A computerized program tracks the students' class credits and provides school records instantly to the new school where the student is registered. Classes are offered on-line, accessible from anywhere the student may be. Summer programs combine part-time work and school. Former migrant students act as mentors and counselors.

# Religion

About 85 percent of Mexicans are Roman Catholics. (To learn more about Roman Catholicism, see page 95 of *The Newest Americans,* Volume 1.) Protestant Christians make up the rest of the population.

Mexican and Mexican American Catholics revere the Virgin of Guadalupe (Gwah-dah-LOO-pay), the patron saint of North America. They offer prayers to her and create shrines in her honor. Because the Virgin resembles both the European version of Mary and an Indian goddess, Mexicans believe that she represents the birth of a new people—the mestizo.

## The Virgin of Guadalupe

Ten years after the Spanish defeated the Aztecs, a vision of the Virgin appeared before Juan Diego, a poor Amerindian. Speaking to him in his native language, she asked him to tell the church leaders to build a church on the spot where she stood. When the bishop demanded proof, Juan Diego brought him a cloakful of roses that the Virgin had made bloom on the hillside. An image of the Virgin was imprinted on the cloak. A church was built on the site in the 1500s and was replaced with a larger church in the 1990s. The faithful still visit the site to see the cloak with the image of the Virgin and to pray. In 2002, Juan Diego was canonized by Pope John Paul II, becoming the first Mexican Indian saint.

## Holidays and Festivals

From Cinco de Mayo (SEEN-ko duh MAH-yoh) to Las Posadas (lahs poh-SAH-dahs), Mexico's festivals and celebrations have long been celebrated in America.

## Heritage Festivals

Cinco de Mayo, the Fifth of May, celebrates the defeat of French troops by the poorly armed and outnumbered citizens of Puebla, Mexico, in 1862. Americans began to celebrate Cinco de Mayo in the 1970s. Many communities have parades and festivals featuring Mexican folk music and dances. Mexicans and Mexican Americans also celebrate Mexico's Independence Day on September 16.

While traditional American Columbus Day celebrations on October 12 focus on Christopher Columbus's discovery of the Americas, the day has a different meaning for Latinos. Called Dia de la Raza (DEE-ah-day-lah-RAH-zah), or Day of Our Race, this day recognizes the impact of European colonization on their culture. While some people celebrate the creation of the mestizo race and culture from the combination of the Spanish and indigenous cultures, others reflect upon the devastation of cultures caused by colonization.

## Religious Holidays

### Día de los Muertos

One of Mexico's most unique holidays, Día de los Muertos (DEE-ahday-lohs-MWAIR-tohs) is celebrated on November 2. The Day of the Dead is an ancient celebration, originating with the people who lived in Mexico over 3,000 years before the Spanish arrived. It is based on the belief that death is a part of life and that spirits interact with the living. When Catholic missionaries couldn't eliminate the holiday, they combined it with the Christian observance of All Souls' Day. Many Mexicans and Mexican Americans continue this tradition in their American homes.

*Elementary school students, parents, and people from the community begin a procession through Chicago celebrating the tradition of Día de los Muertos. Some of the participants carry* Mojigangas *made of papier-mâché similar to those used in processions in Mexico.*

Families set up altars in their homes to honor family members who have died. Photos of the family member and photos or statues of saints are placed on the altar, which also holds the favorite foods and drink of the deceased and a special bread called *pan de muertos*. Flowers, candles, skeleton dolls, and skulls made of sugar or wood decorate the altar.

On November 2, families gather in front of the altar to reminisce, sharing stories about the dead and listening to their favorite music. Some cities have citywide celebrations on the weekend closest to November 2. Businesses and community centers raise awareness of community issues by setting up altars honoring victims of gang violence or drunken driving. Parades with people dressed in skeleton costumes, dancers, and musicians draw people from many cultures to the joyful celebration of life and death.

## Las Posadas

Las Posadas commemorates Joseph and Mary's search for a place to stay before Jesus' birth in Bethlehem. (*Posada* means "lodging," but the celebration honors Joseph and Mary's journey.) Between December 16 and Christmas Day, friends and families visit each other's homes. They share traditional foods and good conversation. Caroling (singing Christmas songs) is another favorite activity during this time. Some churches in America host a community-wide procession, reenacting Joseph and Mary's search for housing. A church service and Christmas carols complete the evening.

## Christmas

Mexicans bring many Christmas traditions with them to America in addition to Las Posadas. Weekends leading up to Christmas are set aside to make tamales (tah-MAH-lays), a traditional Christmas dish. Luminarias (loo-mee-NAH-ree-ahs), candles set inside paper bags to create lanterns, line sidewalks and decorate yards, inviting friends to visit.

On Christmas Eve, many Mexicans attend midnight mass. A family meal with everyone's favorite traditional foods, including the tamales they labored to make, is served on Christmas. Although most children in Mexico receive their gifts on January 6, the Day of the Three Kings, most children in America have adopted the Christmas gift-giving traditions that are common in this country.

# The Arts

### Visual Arts

Mexican Americans have enriched their communities with traditional arts that have been adapted to their lives in the United States. For example, many Mexican Americans have tapped into the tradition of creating public works of art, such as murals, by painting elaborate scenes on their cars and trucks.

Mexican American painters continue the tradition of muralists such as Diego Rivera in America as well. One California artist, Judith Baca, has worked with juvenile offenders to create a mural half a mile (0.8 kilometers) long showing the multiethnic history of the Los Angeles area. Other artists are combining traditional Mexican art styles and images with modern scenes and techniques to produce paintings that represent the Chicano and Mexican experience in America.

*This Chevrolet delivery van took more than three years to customize for the "lowrider" show circuit. Lowriders are cars that have been lowered to almost street level and have been a part of the Mexican culture since the 1930s.*

### Music

When asked about Mexican music, most Americans think of mariachis (mair-ee-AH-chees), musicians wearing large sombreros who perform in Mexican restaurants and at fiestas. Although the mariachi tradition is very important to Mexicans and Mexican Americans, they enjoy many other types of music as well.

Before the 1900s, *corridos* (koh-REE-dohs) were enjoyed throughout the American Southwest. *Corridos* are traditional Mexican folk songs and ballads. The Mexicans working in America, as well as those who became Mexican Americans when the border shifted, sang *corridos* that described their experiences living and working in America. One famous song told of a Mexican immigrant being hanged for a murder that he didn't commit.

*Conjunto* (kon-HOON-toh) music originated in Texas in the early twentieth century. During the Mexican Revolution, many German, Czech, and Polish immigrants fled Mexico and settled in south Texas. Over time, Mexican musicians incorporated the waltz and polka rhythms of these European settlers into their traditional *corridos*. They also added a European instrument—the accordion—to the traditional guitar and drum. By the 1920s, *conjunto* music was popular throughout the region.

By the 1950s, popular musicians began combining *conjunto* with country-western music. With lyrics generally sung in Tex-Mex, a mixture of Spanish and English, the new style was labeled Tejano music. Influenced by the pop and rhythm and blues sounds of the 1960s and 1970s, Tejano music developed an orchestra sound. Keyboards were added in the 1980s, an influence of the disco era. It remains popular throughout Texas and the southwestern United States today.

*Popular Mexican American singer Selena performs at the Cunningham Elementary School in Corpus Christi, Texas, in 1994.*

## Spotlight on
### SELENA

By the age of twenty-three, Selena Quintanilla-Perez had become the undisputed queen of Tejano music. Her charismatic stage performances, combined with her down-to-earth friendliness, grabbed the attention of music producers as well as fans.

Born in Lake Jackson, Texas, in 1971 to Mexican American parents, Selena grew up speaking English. When she began singing with her father's band, Los Dinos, at the age of eight, Selena had to learn the Spanish lyrics phonetically. She later became a fluent Spanish speaker.

Selena was a frequent winner at the Tejano Music Awards, beginning with her first award—Female Vocalist of the Year—in 1987. Over the next ten years, she won the awards for both Female Vocalist of the Year and Female Entertainer of the Year for nine straight years, as well as numerous other awards. Selena also won a Grammy Award in 1993 for Best Mexican American/Tejano Music Performance.

Selena died on March 31, 1995, murdered by a business associate who had been accused of embezzling money. She is still honored and admired by millions of fans who were inspired by her accomplishments.

## Food

The Spanish conquerors found many new and delicious foods when they arrived in Mexico. Pumpkins, turkey, and sweet potatoes are all native to Mexico. Corn, rice, and beans are staples in the Mexican diet; many families eat them every day. Tortillas (tor-TEE-yahs), a type of round, flat bread, are eaten at every meal. They are usually made from corn in southern Mexico and from wheat flour in northern states.

*Mole poblano,* turkey cooked in a sauce made from chiles, sesame seeds, herbs and spices, and unsweetened chocolate, is considered the national dish of Mexico. It is often served on special occasions such as Christmas. Many families also place it as an offering on the family altar during Día de los Muertos.

Tacos are probably the most popular Mexican food in America. They originated when women would wrap the meat or beans for their husband's lunch in tortillas to make it easier to carry to the field. American tacos don't bear much resemblance to the tacos sold in Mexico, however. Few Mexican tacos are fried; none use the pre-formed, hard corn shells that are popular in the United States.

**Did you know?**

Taco stands in Mexico City sell some types of tacos in the morning and other types in the evening. No tacos are sold from street carts between noon and six P.M.

Ingredients and food preparation techniques of northern Mexico and southern Texas combined to produce the Tex-Mex style of cooking. These dishes usually feature beef and cheese. In recent years, restaurants serving traditional foods from the interior of Mexico and the Yucatán Peninsula have had great success in American cities.

## Guacamole

4 ripe avocados

1 large ripe tomato, chopped

1/2 cup onion, finely chopped

2 or more jalapeño or serrano peppers, seeded and finely chopped

Lime juice to taste

Salt to taste

Peel and seed avocados. Place in a glass or plastic bowl. (Note: Using a metal bowl will cause the avocados to turn brown very quickly.) Mash with a fork. Stir in remaining ingredients. If not serving immediately, place the avocado seeds in the guacamole to help keep it from turning brown.

Serves 4 to 8.

# CHAPTER TWO

Nicaraguans

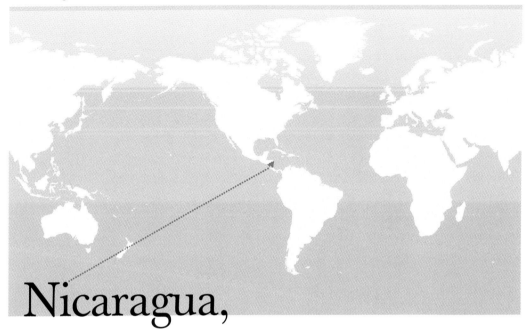

# Nicaragua,

a large country in Central America, has struggled to rebuild after years of civil war and natural disasters devastated the region. Rebuilding remains a challenge, though. Poverty is widespread, and recent droughts are threatening food sources.

There are three main *ethnic groups* in Nicaragua. Mestizos, people of mixed Spanish and Indian ancestry, make up the largest group, with about 69 percent of the population. They live primarily in western Nicaragua. Eastern Nicaragua is home to Creoles, people of mixed African, European, and Indian ancestry, and the Miskito, a group of indigenous people. The Creoles and Miskito generally speak English well, due to the influence of an English presence in the region during the seventeenth, eighteenth, and nineteenth centuries.

Due to the mountainous geography of Nicaragua, these groups rarely interact with each other. The same holds true when they settle in America.

## A Quick Look Back

When Spanish conquerors arrived in western Nicaragua early in the sixteenth century, they quickly overpowered the indigenous people living there. Under Spanish rule, Nicaragua became part of the Kingdom of Guatemala. Guatemala and Mexico together formed the Viceroyalty of New Spain. Because Nicaragua was so far away from the governmental centers, it was neglected somewhat by Spain. Taking advantage of the situation, British colonists settled along the eastern coast of Nicaragua in the 1600s. This region became known as the Mosquito Coast, after the Miskito people who lived in the region.

Nicaragua, Mexico, and other Central American countries declared their independence from Spain in 1821. They briefly united as the Mexican Empire, but Nicaragua, Guatemala, Costa Rica, El Salvador, and Honduras split off to form the United Provinces of Central America in 1823. The federation, marked by struggles for power between conservative and liberal factions, dissolved in 1838, and Nicaragua became an independent country.

## American Interest

With the discovery of gold in California in 1849, people in the eastern part of the United States began searching for a shortcut to the Pacific Ocean. They soon focused on Nicaragua as a possible solution. The Nicaraguan government gave the United States permission to create a route across Nicaragua. While plans called for a canal to connect the Caribbean to the Pacific Ocean, an overland route would be used first. In return for this concession, the United States promised to protect Nicaragua if Britain tried to colonize the country. However, when Britain tried to block the United States from using the overland route, the two countries negotiated a solution without any input from the Nicaraguan government. They agreed that Britain would control the seaports, while the United States would control the land transportation and the hotels and restaurants along the route.

Meanwhile, conflicts between Nicaragua's conservatives and liberals had escalated into civil war. Generally, Nicaragua's wealthiest and most powerful citizens identified themselves as conservatives. They wanted to maintain the status quo, including a strong role for the Roman Catholic Church. Liberals, on the other hand, while also among the privileged, believed that the power of the Catholic Church should be limited. They sought to institute a public education system and social reforms that addressed the concerns of the poor.

In 1855, as the conservatives gained power, the liberals sought the help of William Walker, a well-known American with ambition to control and annex new territories for the United States. Walker brought his own army into the country

*This portrait of William Walker dates from about 1856 during the time he was the dictator of Nicaragua.*

and soon controlled both the conservatives and liberals. Walker declared himself president and ruled over Nicaragua for two years before troops from Nicaragua and other Central American countries joined forces to remove him from power.

In the last few years of the nineteenth century, Nicaragua made many strides economically. Coffee became a leading export, and railroads were built to make the transport of products more efficient. Foreign countries were encouraged to invest in Nicaragua, an offer which American businesses were quick to accept. By the end of the century, Americans controlled most of the banana, coffee, gold, and lumber industries. The British finally withdrew from the Mosquito Coast, leaving Nicaragua in control of the entire country for the first time in its history.

## Military Intervention

Nicaragua's political instability continued through the next decade, with one president after another overthrown or forced to resign. Several presidents requested U.S. military assistance; as a result, U.S. Marines were posted in Nicaragua almost continuously until 1933.

The conservatives held power during most of this period. When the violence of liberal rebels escalated, the United States negotiated a peace agreement. In 1926, both sides agreed to put down weapons and work together to build the Nicaraguan National Guard—a military that was not controlled by either side. The U.S. Marines would provide the training for the new military group.

Juan Bautista Sacasa and Augusto César Sandino, rebel leaders who strongly opposed any U.S. involvement in Nicaragua, denounced the treaty and refused to sign it. Sacasa briefly left the country in protest, while General Sandino led peasants and mine workers in *guerrilla* attacks against the U.S. troops in the region.

Following two relatively peaceful and honest Nicaraguan elections, the United States withdrew its troops in 1933. Juan Bautista Sacasa had just been elected president. He appointed

Anastasio Somoza García to head the National Guard, a move that would prove his downfall.

When President Sacasa took office, he signed a truce with General Sandino and his guerrillas. Sandino, however, believed that the National Guard was unconstitutional because of the role played by the United States in its creation. He continued to push for the National Guard to be abolished. Somoza reacted by arranging the assassination of Sandino by National Guard officers in 1934.

With the National Guard firmly under his control, Somoza began consolidating his power. He forcibly replaced officials who supported President Sacasa with his own allies. In 1936, Sacasa resigned the presidency under pressure from Somoza, setting the stage for Somoza's election to the presidency later that year. (Although Somoza held elections periodically, they were always rigged to result in a victory for Somoza or his selected candidate. Voters had to tell election workers which candidate they were voting for. National Guard soldiers were stationed at the polling places to pick up the ballots as each person voted. People who worked in factories owned by Somoza, which was a large percentage of the population, were fired if they voted for anyone but Somoza.)

## Sandinistas

General Augusto César Sandino led the poorest of Nicaragua's people in a rebellion against social inequality and U.S. intervention in the 1920s. He was executed by Anastasio Somoza García, then head of the National Guard, in 1934. In the 1960s, groups of rebels joined forces to challenge the government of Somoza's son Anastasio Somoza Debayle. They called themselves *Sandinistas* in honor of Sandino's efforts to empower the people of Nicaragua.

## The Somoza Years

Somoza used the power of the government to build his family's immense wealth. Over time, the Somoza family bought real estate, factories, broadcasting companies, and other businesses. Most Nicaraguans believe that the properties were virtually stolen from their previous owners, a charge that the remaining members of the Somoza family vehemently deny. Somoza used the power of the National Guard to silence anyone who spoke out against his government. Opponents were *exiled*, thrown into prison, tortured, or killed. Despite these abuses, the United States continued to support Somoza because he was able to provide a stable environment for American businesses operating in Nicaragua and because he shared an anti-*Communist* philosophy.

Although Somoza bowed to pressure from the United States to hold elections in 1947, he handpicked the candidates; the decisions made by the so-called puppet presidents were actually made by Somoza. Deals made with conservative leaders helped Somoza win the 1950 presidential election once again.

When Somoza was assassinated in 1956, his son Luis assumed the presidency. (Somoza had changed the *constitution* to allow Luis to succeed him in the event of his sudden death.) Luis's brother, Anastasio Somoza Debayle, served as head of the National Guard. The brothers continued to cooperate with the United States, even providing support for the Bay of Pigs invasion against Cuba in 1961. The economy expanded, but only those who were already wealthy saw any benefit. The poor continued to grow poorer.

During the 1960s, a small group of rebels began making plans to oust the Somozas. They called themselves the Sandinista National Liberation Front (Spanish acronym FSLN) in honor of General Augusto Sandino, who had fought to empower poor Nicaraguans forty years earlier. The Sandinistas believed that Nicaragua should adopt a socialist government, one which owns all businesses and controls the economy. The movement gained strength through the 1960s as peasants and students joined the rebel group.

By 1970, most Nicaraguans were struggling to make a living and feed their families. Education and health care were limited for all but the wealthy. As conditions worsened, more people joined the Sandinistas, whose guerrilla attacks against the government increased and became more successful. The National Guard retaliated with strikes against villages and towns throughout the country. Many innocent civilians were killed and tortured.

The international community began to realize just how corrupt the government was after a massive earthquake in 1972 nearly leveled the capital city of Managua. Although up to 10,000 people died and hundreds of thousands were left homeless, the Somoza family took advantage of the tragedy to make even more money, inflating the prices of building materials and supplies. The National Guard looted businesses and homes. Both the Somoza family and the National Guard were also accused of putting the money intended for the earthquake victims into their own bank accounts and selling donated supplies such as medicine and food to the people who needed them. The Somoza family has denied these accusations.

# Anastasio Somoza García

Anastasio Somoza García came to power with close ties to both the liberals and the United States. A nephew of President Sacasa, Somoza was educated in the United States, where he learned English and picked up American customs. Somoza participated in the Nicaraguan National Guard training that was provided by the U.S. Marines. Because of his experiences in America and his outgoing personality, Somoza made many friends in the U.S. military both in Nicaragua and America.

By the time the United States withdrew from Nicaragua in 1933, Somoza had been named head of the National Guard. When he was elected president in 1936 after forcing President Sacasa to resign, Somoza relied upon the political support of friends in the U.S. government and the power of the National Guard to help him remain in office.

Nicaragua made several positive advances during Somoza's rule. The *economy* grew, enabling Nicaragua to pay off all foreign debt. Social programs extended workers' rights and established a social security program. Women were given the right to vote. Despite these accomplishments, most remember Somoza for the culture of corruption and fear that he established during the twenty years that he controlled Nicaragua's government.

## Growing Outrage

The actions of the Somoza family following the earthquake outraged the world. Middle- and upper-class Nicaraguans began supporting the Sandinistas as they stepped up their guerrilla attacks. The Roman Catholic Church spoke out against the Somoza regime's terror campaigns in the countryside. Support for Somoza's government from the United States weakened, especially after Jimmy Carter was elected president in 1976.

*The President of Nicaragua, Anastasio Somoza García (1896-1956).*

# The Sandinistas

In 1978, widespread rioting and protests broke out after the assassination of Pedro Joaquin Chamorro, a newspaper editor who frequently criticized Somoza's government. The Sandinistas stepped up their attacks, taking the entire Nicaraguan congress hostage in August. Soon Nicaragua was engulfed in civil war as the Sandinistas and the National Guard battled for control of the country.

As the fighting escalated, the pressure grew for Somoza to resign from office. Finally, in July 1979, Somoza and his family fled the country. Several officers of the National Guard sought asylum in neighboring countries.

The Sandinistas took control of Nicaragua's government. They planned programs that would address the health and education needs of the poor. Land reforms—taking land away from wealthy landowners and distributing it among the poor—were also planned. Although members of the business community who were not Sandinistas had been included in the temporary legislature, they did not endorse a complete change to socialism. Neither did many citizens.

## The Contras Fight Back

After a brief period of relative peace, civil war erupted again in the early 1980s. This time the rebels were called the Contras, or counterrevolutionaries. The Contras were supported by the United States because they were seen as fighting the spread of *Communism*. (Socialism, the form of government endorsed by the Sandinistas, is considered the first step toward Communism.) The United States also placed a trade embargo, or ban on trade, on Nicaragua. In turn, the Sandinista government began accepting military aid from the Soviet Union and Cuba.

By the late 1980s, the situation in Nicaragua had deteriorated terribly. Food shortages were widespread, and the food that was available was too expensive for most families. The civil war escalated as the United States increased its military support for the Contras. The economic changes put into place by the Sandinistas resulted in exorbitant inflation rates—estimated at one point at 36,000 percent. The Soviet Union had been providing financial and military aid to the Sandinistas, but that diminished throughout the 1980s as its own economy declined. Finally, in 1988, the Sandinistas and the Contras agreed to begin peace talks, although the war didn't end immediately.

As the peace talks continued into 1989, the United Nations sent a peace-keeping force to Nicaragua. The Sandinista government, led by Daniel Ortega, agreed to hold presidential elections in 1990 under the supervision of international observers. Although the Sandinistas were confident that Ortega would be easily reelected, Violeta Barrios de Chamorro, the National Opposition Union candidate and widow of assassinated newspaper editor Pedro Joaquin Chamorro, won with a startling 55 percent of the vote.

During her term in office, Chamorro managed to bring inflation under control and end the military draft. The constitution was revised to give the legislature more power and to place the military under civilian control. However, the continuing economic slump and lack of jobs contributed to an increase in violent crime.

The international community responded with a massive relief effort. Many countries cancelled Nicaragua's debts. In the United States, Nicaraguans who were in the country illegally were allowed to remain temporarily.

## Inflation

What does inflation mean in real life? In 1988 in Nicaragua, it meant that rice cost about $4 per pound. Many families could not earn enough money to feed themselves, even when every-one, adults and children, worked. (In comparison, in 2002 in the United States, a pound of rice cost about 20 cents.)

## Nicaragua Today

Nicaragua is still struggling to overcome the damage done by years of civil war, a devastating hurricane in 1998, and earthquakes in 2000. Although food shortages are a thing of the past, many Nicaraguans are unemployed and can't afford to buy what is in the stores. Instead, they try to grow enough corn and beans to feed their families. An extended drought in 2001 and 2002, followed by flooding in 2002, has decimated the crops, however, leaving many people malnourished and hungry.

Enrique Bolaños, a member of the Liberal Constitutionalist Party, was elected president in 2001. He began his term by investigating charges of corruption against former president Alemán. Alemán's current position as leader of the National Assembly has given him immunity from prosecution, but many Nicaraguans are pressuring representatives to remove Alemán from office so the case can be taken to trial.

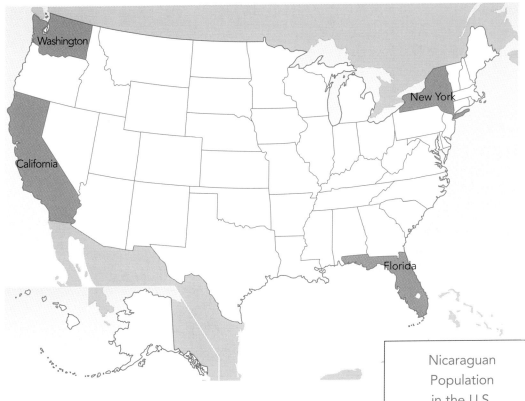

| Nicaraguan Population in the U.S. | |
| --- | ---: |
| Florida | 116,001 |
| California | 74,278 |
| New York | 8,583 |
| Washington | 8,043 |

*Source: U.S. Census, 2000*

## Coming to America

A merica and Nicaragua have been linked together by economic and political concerns for over a century. During this time, many affluent Nicaraguans sent their children to be educated in the United States. During the 1950s, one of the earliest Nicaraguan communities in Miami was established by Creole people from the southern Atlantic coast of Nicaragua. It wasn't until the end of the Somoza dynasty, however, that Nicaraguans began *immigrating* in large numbers to the United States.

The first of these *immigrants* were middle- and upper-class Nicaraguans who did not support either the excesses of the Somoza government or the Communist policies of the Sandinistas. Those who

### U.S./Nicaraguan Immigration by Decade

| Decade | Immigrants |
| --- | --- |
| 1971–80 | 13,004 |
| 1981–90 | 44,139 |
| 1991–2000 | 97,713 |

*Source:* Statistical Yearbook of the Immigration and Naturalization Service

arrived before 1980 generally entered as immigrants, rather than *refugees,* and were absorbed into their new communities without much fuss. As professionals and entrepreneurs, they adapted fairly easily to their new life in America.

During the Sandinistas' rule (1979–1990), about 10 percent of Nicaragua's population fled to other countries. In the United States, the two most popular destinations were Florida and California. The hostile reception Nicaraguans received in Miami surprised them. While Cubans—who also fled a Communist regime—were nearly always granted asylum and given refugee benefits, Nicaraguans had their claims denied time after time. Many felt betrayed by the very country that represented democracy and freedom.

The 1996 Illegal Immigration Reform and Immigrant Responsibility Act expanded the penalties for entering the United States illegally. Up to 40,000 Nicaraguans in the Miami area alone were threatened with deportation. A group of Nicaraguan immigrants sued the federal government, claiming that they were being treated unfairly. This led to a temporary restraining order on deportations of Nicaraguans.

In 1997, President Bill Clinton signed the Nicaraguan Adjustment and Central American Relief Act (NACARA). This law provided eligible Nicaraguans an opportunity to become permanent legal residents if they had been living in the United States continuously since December 1995. (Anyone who was not eligible under the Immigration and Nationality Act, such as a convicted felon, was not eligible under NACARA either.)

When Hurricane Mitch devastated Nicaragua in 1998, the United States granted Temporary Protected Status (TPS) to many Nicaraguans. Under TPS, they were protected from deportation. They also became eligible for a work permit. TPS is not an automatic path to permanent resident status, however. When the TPS expires, Nicaraguans will revert to their original status. This means that those who were illegal and subject to deportation before TPS was granted will once again be subject to deportation when it ends.

### Nicas

Nicaraguans often refer to themselves as "Nicas."

By 2000, about 280,000 Nicaraguans were living in America; approximately 25 percent were here illegally. In the Miami-Dade County metropolitan area, Nicaraguans were the second largest Hispanic group.

# Life in America

Nicaraguans, for the most part, have had a difficult time finding success in America. Many are in the country illegally, which affects every aspect of their lives. Drawn by images of plentiful jobs and an easier life, thousands risk their lives to travel through Honduras or El Salvador, Guatemala, and Mexico to reach the United States. Once here, they find that–without legal documents and the ability to speak English–jobs are difficult to find and keep. And the jobs they do get don't pay very well. Both parents often work, and many hold down two jobs in order to pay for housing and food. The dream of moving to America and living a life like that shown on television and in the movies rarely comes true.

Unlike many immigrant groups in America, Nicaraguans have formed few organizations to offer support to new immigrants. In part, this is due to the uncertain legal status of many Nicaraguans. It is also indicative of the independent nature of most Nicaraguans.

In surveys of immigrant children and their parents, Nicaraguans have reported more instances of *discrimination* than any other group. The discrimination can be caused by several factors, most importantly the lack of legal status and resulting poverty. Many children describe themselves as "Hispanic" in order to distance themselves from the stigma of "Nicaraguan." After a few years in America, however, some children reclaim their ethnic heritage with pride.

## Family

Nicaraguan families, like many in Latin America, are very close. It is not unusual for extended families to immigrate together and to share the same house in America. Women are traditionally responsible for the care of the children and the home, although when they immigrate to America they are often forced to work outside the home to support the family. They do not give up their responsibilities at home, though; few Nicaraguan men help out with child care or housework.

Nicaraguan families are more likely than other Latino immigrants to speak Spanish in the home. On the whole, Nicaraguan parents feel that their children need to understand and be proud of their Nicaraguan heritage, even as they adapt to life in the United States.

Those who are in America illegally have other concerns as well. Many neglect their health because they are afraid that they will be deported, or sent back to Nicaragua, if they seek medical care. This is especially true in California, where Proposition 187, passed in 1994, required doctors and other health care officials, as well as teachers and social service providers, to verify the immigration status of each client and report illegal immigrants to the Immigration and Naturalization Service (INS). Although the law has been tied up in the courts and has not been implemented yet, many parents are still afraid to visit a medical clinic.

*This family of refugees from Nicaragua has lived in the United States for more than fifteen years. They are eligible for permanent residence status under the Nicaraguan Adjustment and Central American Relief Act passed by Congress in 1997.*

## Work

Although about one-third of the immigrants from Nicaragua were professionals and business owners in their country, relatively few work in a professional environment in America. The language barrier and the illegal status of many immigrants have kept most Nicaraguans in low-paying, dead-end jobs. It is not unusual to find janitors, factory workers, or lab technicians who were employed as engineers, scientists, and teachers before leaving Nicaragua. Many speak of the frustration they feel knowing that they have the skills and training to succeed in the United States, but are unable to capitalize on their abilities because of their illegal status.

In Miami, some women cook traditional foods such as *nacatamales* (nah-cah-tah-MAH-lees) and sell them to neighborhood eateries or to other Nicaraguans who crave the taste of food from their homeland. In a way, this work continues a tradition from Nicaragua where those who had an oven often sold tortillas to families who had no oven.

Another cottage industry, or work produced at home, is related to Nicaraguan celebrations. Some immigrants make dance costumes for processions and folk dance troupes, while others create decorations for weddings, baptisms, communions, and holidays. Nicaraguan piñatas are also created and sold by Nicaraguan artists.

*A young man takes a swing at a piñata while attending a birthday party.*

## School

The educational experience of Nicaraguan students in America varies greatly. Most school-age children of middle- to upper-income Nicaraguans had attended school in their home country before coming to America. Poor children and those living in rural areas had few educational opportunities until the Sandinistas took control of the country. Even under the Sandinistas, there was a shortage of teachers and a lack of resources in the schools. Many students had to work to help support their families. Regardless of background, however, Nicaraguan students feel fortunate to have the opportunity to attend school in America.

Many Nicaraguan parents hesitate to get involved in their children's schools. They may not be able to get time off from work, or they may feel that they don't speak English well enough to deal with the teachers and other school officials. In spite of this, the parents are deeply involved in their children's lives. They keep track of their friends and activities, hoping to prevent involvement in drugs and gangs.

The parents' limited English skills also prevent them from helping with homework as much as they would like to. They know that education is the key to success in America. Yet they worry that they will not be able to afford to send their children to college or that children will not be able to attend because of their legal status.

The discrimination that Nicaraguan students in Miami face comes mostly from Cuban students, who make up the majority of students in most schools attended by Nicaraguans. Nicaraguan students are called "Indians" and accused of being dirty. Just as the U.S. government made it clear that Nicaraguans would not receive political asylum the way other refugees from Communist governments did, the other students let the Nicaraguans know that "they don't belong." Many newcomers simply ignore the peer discrimination and focus on completing their education.

Those who have been in America longer tend to adopt the label "Latino" or "Hispanic" and speak English rather than Spanish. (Nicaraguan Spanish differs somewhat from Cuban and other Spanish dialects. By speaking English instead of Spanish, Nicaraguan students can eliminate audio cues that betray their ethnic identity and lead to discrimination or ostracism.) Their grades may begin to slip as they spend more energy trying to fit in with their peers. This increased social acceptance comes at a cost, however; usually increased conflict with parents.

Those Nicaraguan students who arrived in America as babies or who were born in America do not usually experience the same level of discrimination as other Nicaraguan students. They fit in more readily and typically claim their Nicaraguan American heritage.

## Religion

The churches that serve Nicaraguan immigrants in America provide many important services. They may help immigrants find jobs or testify for them at asylum hearings. Most importantly, they help the immigrants maintain some of their cultural traditions.

About 85 percent of Nicaraguans are Catholic. The others are Protestant Christians. Many of the Protestants are from the Miskito ethnic group, which lives on the east coast of Nicaragua. They belong to the Moravian church, one of the earliest Protestant churches in the world. The Moravian church got its name from Moravia, the country where it originated. (Today, the country is called the Czech Republic.) Its official name is the Unity of Brethren Church. Missionaries established churches along Nicaragua's Mosquito Coast.

The Moravian churches of Miami serve large communities of Creole and Miskito immigrants. Some church services are conducted in the Miskito language. In addition, the church band may feature traditional Miskito instruments, including drums and other rhythm instruments.

*Celebrants burn incense as others carry a statue of the Virgin of the Assumption (Virgen de la Asuncion) during of one of the most popular religious festivals among Nicaraguans.*

## Holidays and Festivals

As Christians, Nicaraguans celebrate many of the same holidays as Americans, Easter and Christmas chief among them. Other uniquely Nicaraguan celebrations have been brought to America as well.

### Patronal Festivals

Catholics in Nicaragua celebrate the saint day of their town's patron saint with a procession and other events that may last up to three months. These events have been adapted to America and form the basis of some of the community's most exciting celebrations. Most of the planning is done by small businesses or professional organizations. Instead of being held over several days, in America the saint day celebrations, or patronal festivals, are scheduled for the Sunday that is closest to the actual saint day. They are often held in parks or reception halls, and the procession is changed to fit the space available.

Instead of fireworks, those attending the festival may pop hundreds of balloons at the same time. While the church mass is included as part of the American celebration, many other events, such as the folk dances, have to be cut back because of time constraints. Possibly the biggest change, though, is not celebrating all of the patronal festivals. With immigrants from so many towns, this isn't possible. Instead, only the largest or best-known festivals are celebrated in America.

## Purísima

The most widely celebrated patronal festival in Miami is that of the Virgen de la Asuncion. During this festival season, which lasts from November 26 through January, private parties called Purísimas (poo-REE-see-mahs) are held.

Hosts set up altars in their front yards on weekend evenings and invite guests to say the rosary and sing in honor of the Virgin Mary. In return, the guests are fed traditional dishes. They also receive *el paquete*–small gifts of fruit and sweets. Nicaraguans often take turns hosting the Purísimas because of the expense involved for the host. La Griteria, the public celebration of the festival, is usually held on the Sunday closest to December 7. Churches may hold outdoor services and host large groups of carolers. Many businesses also set up altars.

## Moravian Celebrations

Most Moravian celebrations take place in the church, with a special mass and the singing of hymns. The Harvest festival, for example, is held in November. Members place fruits and vegetables, both fresh and home-canned, along with baked goods, plants, and flowers at the altar. Sugarcane and palm leaves decorate the church. During the service, special Harvest hymns are sung. After the service, the items are auctioned off. Church members join together for a festive dinner of traditional foods following the auction.

During Advent, the four weeks before Christmas, most church members make or buy a paper Moravian star and hang it over their porch light. A candlelight service is usually held on Christmas Eve.

On New Year's Eve, Moravian church members observe Watch Night. They gather together in the sanctuary to welcome the New Year by singing hymns all night.

# The Arts

Poetry is a national obsession in Nicaragua. Newspapers issue poetry supplements weekly. Poets are often stopped on the street and asked for their autographs, much as athletes and actors are in the United States. According to Yolanda Blanco, a contemporary Nicaraguan poet who lives in New York City, the great poets of her country are Nicaragua's heroes.

## *Spotlight on*
### GIOCONDA BELLI

*Nicaraguan poet, novelist, and political activist Gioconda Belli reads from her works in New York City in 2002.*

One of Nicaragua's premier poets, Gioconda Belli was born into an upper-class family in 1948. After completing her education, Belli became aware of the social problems crushing Nicaragua's people and joined the Sandinista revolution. Her poetry started appearing in Nicaraguan journals.

In 1972, Belli was awarded the Marino Fiallos Gil Prize for Poetry for her first book, *Sobre la Grama*. Her second poetry collection, *Linea de Fuego* (Line of Fire), won the Casa de las Americas Prize in 1978.

Today Belli writes novels as well as poetry. She divides her time between homes in Nicaragua and Los Angeles.

> **"Every Nicaraguan** is a poet until proven otherwise."
> —Jose Coronel Urtecho

Although Nicaraguans have a strong tradition of hand-crafts, such as embroidered clothing, goldsmithing, and wood-carving, few practice the crafts in America. Many people who fled the country had to leave their tools behind. Others aren't able to save enough money to buy supplies for their crafts. Some crafts and skills, such as boatbuilding, simply aren't needed in Miami or California.

One notable exception is the fabric art of the Creole women. Having learned tatting (lace-making), crochet, and embroidery from the Moravian missionary women, they continue to create beautiful items today. These are generally for personal use, though, and are rarely produced as a means of making money.

## Food

In Nicaragua, most families survive on rice and beans. Corn, avocados, plantains, and chile peppers are other basic foods. However, many people can't afford to buy enough food to feed their families. Because of this widespread poverty, malnutrition is a big problem in Nicaragua.

When Nicaraguans arrive in the United States, they are often amazed at the amount of food available in the super-markets. Having made everything from scratch in Nicaragua, including grinding the corn for cornmeal, the women welcome the convenience of buying ingredients that are ready to cook with. It is also a welcome change to have a refriger-ator, stove, and oven in their homes. Few could afford these appliances in Nicaragua.

Just as Nicaraguans continue to eat their traditional foods in America, they also continue the tradition of sharing the meal with any guests who happen to drop by while the meal is cooked. Some women also cook Nicaraguan corn tortillas, which are slightly thicker than Mexican tortillas, and sell them to neighbors or local Nicaraguan eateries.

Miami has several *fritangas* (free-TAHN-gahs), or Nicaraguan cafeterias. They seldom have tables; customers order their food to go or eat standing up. The cafeterias serve traditional foods, such as fried plantains or nacatamales (meat, rice, and vegetables enclosed in a layer of ground corn and steamed). Although it is traditional to wrap and steam the nacatamales in banana leaves, this can be expensive in the United States. Aluminum foil is often used to save money.

A favorite Nicaraguan breakfast has become a popular snack in Nicaraguan American communities. *Vigoron* (vee-GOR-ohn) is prepared by arranging fried pork rinds on boiled cassava root and topping it with a cabbage and tomato salad. The availability of already prepared pork rinds makes this dish very easy to make in America.

The cooking traditions of the people living in eastern Nicaragua vary somewhat from the mestizo cooking described above. Fish and coconut milk are important ingredients in these dishes. A favorite dish from this region is called "run down" (ron-don). It is made by boiling fish or meat on top of root vegetables grown in the area; the flavor of the meat "runs down" to the vegetables. Coconut is added to the dish as it cooks. Run down is usually served with gallo pinto, a dish of beans and rice. When eastern Nicaraguans prepare gallo pinto, they generally add coconut milk.

Recipe

## Gallo Pinto

*This dish is often called the national dish of Nicaragua. The name means "spotted rooster," but the dish doesn't have any chicken in it! It may be eaten at any meal, although it is most commonly served at dinner.*

2 tablespoons vegetable oil

2 medium onions, chopped

3 cups cooked red beans

2 cups cooked white rice

Optional:

Coconut milk

Red or green peppers, chopped

Cilantro, chopped

Garlic, minced

Hot pepper sauce

Heat the oil in a heavy skillet over medium heat. Add the chopped onions and sauté until they are translucent. Add the beans and rice and fry for several minutes, stirring frequently until the beans and rice begin to get crispy. Serve by itself or with eggs, fruit, or meat.

If desired, coconut milk, red or green peppers, cilantro, or garlic may be added during the cooking. Hot pepper sauce is often added to the dish when it is served.

*Source: Adapted from Citizenship and Immigration Canada, "Eating the Nicaraguan Way,"* Cultural Profiles Project *http://cwr.utoronto.ca/cultural/english/nicaragua/eating.html*

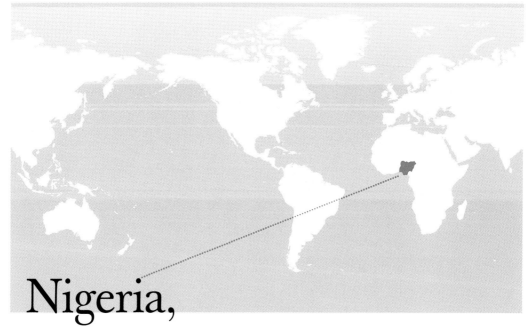

# CHAPTER THREE

# Nigeria,

Africa's most populous country, is home to 130 million people. (By comparison, 288 million people live in the United States.) Over 250 *ethnic groups* and languages are represented in Nigeria. This diversity has led some to call Nigeria "the United States of Africa."

The diverse ethnic groups, lumped together into one country when the region was colonized by Britain, have struggled to see themselves as one nation. The three main ethnic groups have dominated Nigerian politics since independence in 1960. The Hausa-Fulani (HOU-suh FOO-*lah*-nee), the largest group, live primarily in northern Nigeria. Most Yoruba (YOR-uh-buh) live in the southwest, while the majority of Igbo (IG-boh) live in the southeast. Religious as well as ethnic differences have contributed to Nigeria's ongoing political problems, with the north being primarily Islamic and the south Christian.

## Ethnic Groups of Nigeria

| | | |
|---|---|---|
| *a* | Hausa-Fulani | 29% |
| *b* | Yoruba | 21% |
| *c* | Igbo (Ibo) | 18% |
| *d* | Other | 32% |

*Source:* The World Factbook *2002*

## A Quick Look Back

The Yoruba have lived in eastern Nigeria for centuries. They established city-states, territories ruled from the major city in their midst. These city-states were ruled in turn by a royal dynasty. Over time, the Yoruba developed an urbanized society, with artists producing sculptures and metalwork for trade.

In contrast, the Igbo of eastern Nigeria lived in self-sufficient villages. Leaders were chosen for their wisdom, rather than by family lineage. Most people farmed and traded goods at markets.

The northern region was settled first by the Hausa. Their city-states specialized, providing military or religious support for each other. Trade flourished, due to the caravans that crossed the Sahara Desert, exchanging gold and slaves from West Africa for copper and salt in North Africa. The Fulani people moved into Hausaland in the thirteenth century. They were primarily herders, raising cattle, sheep, and goats. Predominantly Muslim, they often acted as advisers to the Hausa leaders and as Islamic teachers and judges.

The Portuguese were the first Europeans to reach West Africa. They arrived in 1471 and set up trading partnerships with the kingdom of Benin (beh-NEEN), one of the Yoruba city-states. Within a few decades, they had begun trading goods for slaves, many of whom were prisoners of war, sold into slavery by their enemies. Most of the slaves were sent to *colonies* in the Americas. Other European countries, attracted by the profitable gold and slave trade, soon joined Portugal in West Africa. By the eighteenth century, Britain dominated the slave trade.

**Did you know?**

It's estimated that by the time the transatlantic slave trade ended in the nineteenth century, over 3.5 million Nigerians had been sold into slavery. Most were Yoruba or Igbo.

## A Century of Changes

The nineteenth century was marked by upheaval and change throughout Nigeria. In 1804, a Fulani leader named Usuman dan Fodio led a jihad (jih-HAHD), or Islamic holy war, against the Hausa in northern Nigeria. In 1808, the conquered Hausa states became part of the newly formed Sokoto Caliphate (SOH-koh-toh KAL-ih-*fate*), or Islamic empire. Fodio's jihad had created the largest empire in Africa since the late 1500s. It also inspired the formation of other Islamic nations in Africa.

While the north was embroiled in a holy war, the British government voted to abolish slave trading in 1807. This decision was primarily due to the growing industrialization of Britain. Manufacturing required far fewer workers than agriculture, but more of Nigeria's raw goods, such as palm oil, were needed.

Pressure from Christian missionaries and freed slaves encouraged Britain to expand its control over other coastal cities from which slaves were shipped. By the end of the nineteenth century, Britain had established a firm presence in southern Nigeria.

## A British Colony

In 1900, the British government established protectorates in southern and northern Nigeria, although force was necessary to bring the north under its control. In 1914, the formation of the Colony and Protectorate of Nigeria brought the three main regions of Nigeria—north, west, and east—together under British rule. Britain implemented a policy of indirect rule. That is, traditional rulers retained control over their regions, but they functioned under the guidance of the British and paid taxes to them. This policy was most successful in the north, where the Hausa-Fulani peoples had a hierarchical system of government in place. As a result, they were able to maintain strong Islamic and traditional values. In contrast, the traditional religions and political structures of ethnic groups in the southern regions were weakened as Western influence spread, both through trade and missionary work.

Many Nigerians pursued higher education in Europe and the United States in the 1920s and beyond. For the most part, they were members of the Nigerian elite, members of the ruling class or former slaves that had returned to Africa. Upon their return in the 1930s and 1940s, they spoke out against colonial rule. These leaders protested the lack of African representation in their government and the racism that kept Nigerians from governing themselves. Many joined nationalist groups that demanded independence for Nigeria. Others pushed for self-rule as a member of the British Commonwealth.

## Push for Independence

After World War II (1939–1945), the pressure on Britain to grant independence to its African colonies grew. Many British citizens questioned the wisdom of maintaining foreign colonies at a time when Britain itself was recovering from the devastation of the war. The Nigerian independence movement became more organized, and Britain began shifting political power to Nigeria in preparation for independence. A number of *constitutions* were written from 1946 to 1957, providing for regional self-government as well as a federal House of Representatives that would make decisions that affected the nation. Political parties formed largely along ethnic-group lines. Until the late 1940s when the Northern People's Congress was formed, the parties mostly represented southern Nigeria's ethnic groups.

The early constitutions before independence established three political regions within Nigeria. Each region had its own legislative body as well as representation at the national level. Ultimate authority still rested in the hands of the British governor. Southern Nigeria was divided into the Eastern and Western Regions, which began self-government in 1957. The Northern Region followed in 1959. Each region struggled to obtain national power. The two southern regions wanted to implement economic policies that would benefit their people, while the leadership in the north wanted to maintain the status quo with little interference from the federal government.

## Nigeria's Early Years

In October 1960, Britain declared Nigeria an independent country within the British Commonwealth. (The Commonwealth includes any former British colony that wishes to continue its association with Britain. Although nations in the Commonwealth maintain full independence, they share economic ties with Britain.) In the first elections, the Northern People's Congress (NPC), which represented the more populous Northern Region, received most of the votes. Its leader, Sir Abubakar Tafawa Balewa, became the first prime minister of Nigeria. Nnamdi Azikiwe, the leader of the Igbo-dominated National Council of Nigeria and the Cameroons (NCNC), became governor-general. The NPC and the NCNC held most of the power in the federal government for the first three years.

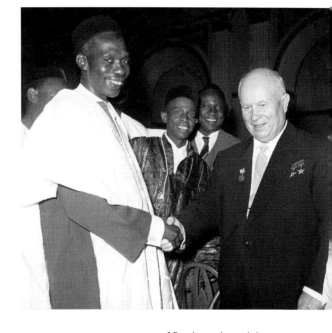

*Nigerian prime minister Abubakar Tafwa Balewa meets Soviet premier Nikita Khrushchev in New York City in 1960.*

The federal government revised the constitution in 1963, declaring Nigeria a republic in the British Commonwealth. As citizens of a republic, Nigerians began electing a president to serve as their head of state rather than a prime minister. (In a parliamentary government, the leader of the political party that has the most elected representatives in the *parliament,* or legislature, becomes the prime minister. A president, on the other hand, is elected independently of the legislative representatives.)

Nigeria's many minority ethnic groups worked hard to gain representation during the early years of Nigeria's independence. A fourth state, the Midwestern Region, was established in 1963 to ensure minority representatives seats in the House of Representatives. However, debate over the creation of several more new states continued. Breaking up the large Northern Region would distribute the power in the government more equally. Opposition groups in the Western Region also hoped that the creation of additional states would limit the influence of the NCNC, which was dominated by Igbo.

By the time the 1964 elections were held, a climate of distrust and suspicion had developed between the various ethnic groups. The Northern Region, predominantly Muslim, was not as economically advanced as the Eastern and Western Regions. Southerners, mostly Christian and Igbo, who worked in northern cities were resented by northern leaders as a threat to their traditional power. The Eastern and Western Regions, on the other hand, did not trust the NPC or each other. The Igbo-led NCNC gained power when it won control of the new Midwestern Region's legislature in 1964, a development that was viewed with dismay by the Western Region.

## Civil War

In January 1966, the Nigerian government was overthrown in a military *coup* led by several Igbo officers. Federal and regional leaders were assassinated. Major General Johnson Aguiyi Ironsi, an Igbo, took control of the government. He banned all political parties, declared the constitution invalid, and appointed his military officers to positions of power within the federal and state governments. Ironsi strongly believed that the country needed to be unified, rather than split into regional and ethnic groups. However, people in other regions assumed that the coup was an attempt by the Igbo to control all of Nigeria and funnel the country's resources to their region.

By June, protests had escalated into violence directed at the Igbo living in the Northern Region. Hundreds of Igbo were killed and their property destroyed. A month later, Hausa and

Fulani army officers led a coup against Ironsi, killing him and many of his officers. Lieutenant Colonel Yakubu "Jack" Gowon was designated as the head of the new military government.

*Lieutenant Colonel Yakubu Gowon shown at age 31 when he assumed power in Nigeria following the Biafran Civil War.*

In early 1967, Gowon's administration divided the four Nigerian states and created twelve new ones, giving more representation to minority groups. The Eastern Region was divided into three new states. This diluted the political strength of the Igbo and cut off their access to the coastal ports and rich oil fields in the region. (Because each region controlled the natural resources of its area, the Igbo had benefited tremendously from oil sales. The creation of the new states left the Igbo with a drastically reduced income.)

Attacks against the Igbo in the Northern Region continued, and by September, thousands of Igbo had been killed. (Some sources say that as many as 30,000 were killed; others say 10,000.) Millions of Igbo fled south, seeking refuge in the Eastern Region—their homeland. Efforts to end the conflict were not successful; the Igbo charged that the Hausa and Fulani had committed genocide, a deliberate attempt to kill everyone of a particular racial or cultural group, in the north. In 1967, the Igbo, led by Lieutenant Colonel Chukwuemeka Odumegwu Ojukwu, voted to secede (separate) from Nigeria and form the Republic of Biafra (bee-AF-ruh).

A bloody, violent, three-year-long war followed. Entire cities in the Eastern Region were destroyed. There was little food or medicine. The small region of Biafra couldn't support all the refugees who were fleeing the terror in the north and west. Estimates of the number who died during the civil war range from 1 million to 3 million.

## After the War

Increased oil production, along with higher oil prices, helped Nigeria's *economy* recover quickly after the civil war. Although there was a lot of money flowing into the country in the early 1970s, most of it found its way to the pockets of an elite few. Industry boomed, as did the development of schools and universities.

Gowon continued to rule as head of the military government after the civil war. The Northern Region was divided into six states, leaving most of the power with the military government. Unemployment rose rapidly in the mid-1970s, especially in the east, where many businesses had been destroyed during the war. Widespread corruption caused scandals involving businesses, government officials, even health providers. Crime rates skyrocketed, as did public executions of criminals.

In 1974, Gowon announced that elections would not be held the next year as planned. Instead, he intended to remain in power six more years. During this time, he planned to reorganize the military, develop a long-range economic plan, create more states, and write a constitution, among other things. Unwilling to wait for change, a group of military officers led by Brigadier Murtala Muhammed took control of the government while Gowon was out of the country. Gowon lived in *exile* in England following the coup.

Murtala Muhammed moved swiftly to oust corrupt government officials and to create a new constitution based on that of the United States. He announced that Nigeria would return to civilian rule when elections were held in 1979. Although Muhammed was assassinated in 1976 in another attempted coup, his successor—Lieutenant General Olusegun Obansanjo—continued to build upon the reforms that Muhammed had begun.

The new constitution introduced many radical changes. Political parties were required to represent national objectives rather than ethnic groups. The president and vice president could not take office unless they received 25 percent of the votes in two-thirds of the states, demonstrating that they were supported by others outside their own ethnic group.

The Nigerian states were divided again to create nineteen states. The divisions increased the number of representatives from minority ethnic groups in an effort to ensure that no one ethnic group could permanently dominate the others. Obansanjo also implemented Muhammed's plans to move the capital from Lagos in southwestern Nigeria to Abuja in the more neutral central region.

## Return to Civilian Rule

Elections were held in 1979. This marked the beginning of what is called the Second Republic of Nigeria—a new government elected under a new constitution. Shehu Shagari was elected president amid high expectations. Increasing revenues from oil development promised to provide the country with enough money to carry out needed programs. New political parties sprang up in the 1980s, but they still formed primarily around ethnic groups.

Oil prices dropped dramatically when the oil market collapsed in the early 1980s, a result of a worldwide recession. Tensions between ethnic groups that had been lying just below the surface rose once more. Riots and protests throughout the country were met with violence from police officers charged with controlling them. Thousands died. Corruption continued in all areas of government and business, and smuggling became one of the major crimes in the nation.

## The Third Republic

A series of military coups in the early 1980s contributed to the ongoing political unrest. Critics of the government were usually arrested. In late 1985, Major General Ibrahim Babangida took control of the government. Referring to himself as president although he was not elected, Babangida loosened some of the restrictions on journalists. The economy continued to decline, however, with unemployment rising and incomes falling. He announced that his *regime* would support the 1979 constitution, with a goal of holding civilian elections in the late 1980s.

In the late 1980s, plans were made for a return once more to civilian rule. This became known as Nigeria's Third Republic. Babangida announced that there would be only two political parties. They would be overseen and financed by the government. In an effort to prevent the parties from aligning along ethnic groups, members had to be recruited throughout the entire country.

### Income

In 1988, the average Nigerian made less than $300 (U.S. dollars).

The Social Democratic Party (SDP) won a majority of seats in the 1992 legislative election. When the presidential election was held in 1993, Moshood Abiola, the SDP candidate, also won easily. However, Babangida and other military leaders did not want the SDP to control the country, and they annulled the election before Abiola could take office. Babangida then announced that he would continue as president.

Faced with riots, protests, and international *sanctions*, Babangida turned the presidency over to an interim president who was promptly overthrown in a coup. General Sani Abacha, the new military leader, put a halt to all political activity. Critics of his government were thrown into prison or executed. Abiola, who had won the 1993 presidential election, was imprisoned and later died in prison. Many Nigerians fled the country for the United States and other destinations. Because of human rights violations under Abacha, Nigeria was removed from the British Commonwealth of Nations.

Abacha finally scheduled presidential elections for 1998. Because he was named as the only candidate for president, though, Nigerians had little hope for reform. However, Abacha died of a heart attack shortly before the elections were to be held.

## Nigeria Today

Abdulsalam Abubakar, a former defense minister, became interim president following Abacha's death in 1998. An investigation later revealed that over $3 billion had been siphoned off by government officials while Abacha controlled the government.

A new constitution was published in 1999 that shifted power to local and state governments. Elections that year placed General Olusegun Obasanjo back in the presidency. He investigated corruption and human rights violations and released political prisoners. After the elections, Nigeria became a member of the British Commonwealth once more.

Nigeria is presently divided into thirty-six states and one federal capital territory. Twelve northern states implemented Shari'a (shah-*ree*-uh), or Islamic, law recently. Harsh punishments such as flogging, amputation, or death by stoning for people who break the law have caused an outcry in the international community. Growing violence between religious and ethnic groups has resulted in the deaths of about 10,000 people since 1999. Talk of creating separate nations for each ethnic group has surfaced as a solution.

The economy continues to suffer under these conditions. Years of coups and fighting have diverted resources away from economic programs. In addition, the population is growing rapidly. As a result, more people are competing for fewer jobs. Schools have not kept pace with the population either; many students are not able to continue their education beyond a basic level.

## Speaking Out

Among those who were imprisoned or executed for daring to speak out against the government were two prominent Nigerian authors. During the Nigerian civil war (1967–1970), Wole Soyinka spent nearly two years in solitary confinement for speaking out in favor of a cease-fire, an experience that he describes in his book *A Man Died*. Soyinka is considered by many to be the greatest African writer of modern times. He has won recognition for his plays, poetry, and novels, including the Nobel Prize for Literature in 1986. When Sani Abacha began suppressing free speech in the early 1990s, Soyinka spoke out against the government once again. This time, Soyinka had to flee Nigeria to avoid a death sentence.

Fellow playwright Ken Saro-Wiwa was not so fortunate. A member of the Ogoni ethnic group in oil-rich southeastern Nigeria, he was involved in the Movement for the Survival of the Ogoni People (MOSOP). Although the Ogoni lands held some of the richest oil reserves, the Ogoni were among the poorest of Nigeria's ethnic groups. Few oil-related jobs were given to Ogoni workers and most of the oil revenue went to more powerful ethnic groups. Meanwhile, oil production caused environmental damage and pollution in the region.

Saro-Wiwa led many protests against the government and the oil companies in 1993 and was arrested many times. In 1994, Saro-Wiwa and eight other activists faced false charges of murder and were given a rushed, unfair trial by Abacha's government. They were executed in 1995.

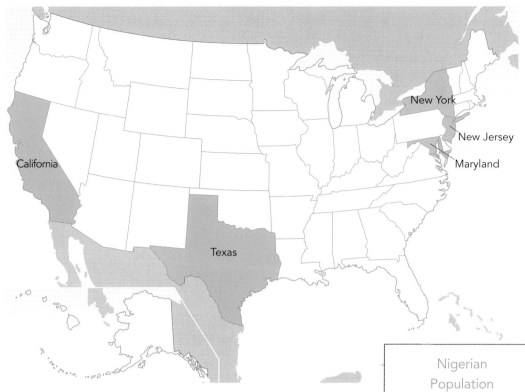

Nigerian Population in the U.S.

| Maryland | 30,810 |
|----------|--------|
| California | 19,645 |
| New York | 14,478 |
| Texas | 13,108 |
| New Jersey | 10,551 |

*Source: U.S. Census, 2000*

# Coming to America

Nigerians have been traveling to the United States on business and to further their education for decades. Some of the most vocal advocates for Nigerian independence were educated in America, including Nnamdi Azikiwe, who founded the National Council of Nigeria and the Cameroons, one of Nigeria's first political parties.

It is only within the past twenty years, however, that Nigerians have immigrated to the United States in large numbers. Before 1965, immigration from Africa was tightly restricted. Once the quotas were eliminated, however, only a few hundred immigrants arrived from Nigeria each year. Nigeria had only recently gained independence from Britain

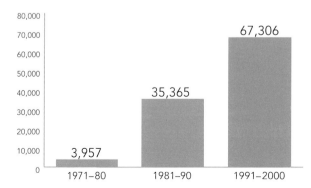

U.S./Nigerian Immigration by Decade

*Source:* Statistical Yearbook of the Immigration and Naturalization Service

(1960) and its citizens were immersed in building their new government. During the civil war (1967–1970), millions of Nigerians were forced from their homes, but few left the country.

The number of immigrants from Nigeria increased steadily through the 1970s and 1980s as political instability and economic problems rocked the country. Many were fleeing political persecution. Most emigrants went to Europe; those who came to America established communities in metropolitan areas such as Washington, D.C., New York City, and Houston, Texas. Most of those who came during this period were professionals. Some were students who, after completing their degrees, decided to stay in America. Many became naturalized citizens.

The 1990s brought nearly double the number of Nigerian immigrants as the previous decade. The Diversity Program, part of the 1990 Immigration Act, provided a boost to Nigerians who hoped to immigrate to America. This program makes extra visas available for immigrants from countries that were underrepresented in the past. Nearly 3,000 Nigerians entered the United States through the Diversity Program in 2000 alone.

The family reunification programs have been important to Nigerian immigrants as well. As more Nigerians become American citizens, they are eligible to bring family members to the United States. In 2000, nearly half of the immigrants from Nigeria were close family members of U.S. citizens.

## *Spotlight on*
### PHILIP EMEAGWALI

When Philip Emeagwali (eh-*may*-ah-gwah-lee) arrived in the United States in 1974, he was seventeen. He had dropped out of school at fourteen. He had never used a computer. But within fifteen years, he had earned the title "Father of the Internet."

Emeagwali grew up in Nigeria as the oldest of nine children. His family was Igbo. They spent the three years of Nigeria's civil war in a refugee camp. Every night his father would challenge him to mentally solve 100 math problems in an hour. He soon became known among his friends as "Calculus." Although he had had to drop out of school because of the war, Emeagwali became a regular at the public library when the war ended. He taught himself college-level math, science, and English. He then took and passed a British equivalency exam that would allow him to attend college.

While working on a problem for his doctoral dissertation in 1989, Emeagwali needed to perform millions of calculations. At the time, the usual method of figuring out complex problems like this was to program a supercomputer, which was prohibitively expensive. Instead, Emeagwali envisioned using 65,000 regular computers, with each working on one aspect of the problem. Scientists around the world were astounded at the results: the networked computers performed 3.1 billion calculations per second, far more than even the most powerful supercomputer could do in that amount of time. The problem he was working on—determining how oil flows underground—was also solved. With this information, oil companies would be able to extract more oil when they drilled, lowering costs and increasing production. Emeagwali's accomplishment earned him the Gordon Bell Prize from the American Institute for Electrical and Electronics Engineers. This prestigious prize is considered to be the Nobel Prize of computing.

The way Emeagwali used the computers to divide the workload yet communicate with each another led other computer scientists to consider the practical aspects of such a system. The resulting computer network was called the Internet, and Philip Emeagwali is considered one of its founding fathers.

Emeagwali often gives speeches to children, encouraging them to excel in school. When he is introduced as a mathematical genius, he tells the story of his father pushing him to excel in mathematics in the refugee camp. He points out that practice and determination contributed to his present success as much as his mathematical abilities.

## *Spotlight on*
### HAKEEM OLAJUWON

Growing up in Lagos, Nigeria, Hakeem Olajuwon (hah-KEEM oh-LIE-juh-wahn) started playing basketball at the age of sixteen. By seventeen, Olajuwon became a member of Nigeria's national junior basketball team. At a tournament, he caught the eye of an American who was coaching basketball in Africa. Soon, Olajuwon was on his way to America. After visiting several colleges in 1980, he enrolled in the University of Houston (UH), in part because the warm weather in Houston reminded him of Nigeria.

In 1984, Olajuwon was the first player chosen in the National Basketball Association (NBA) draft. He became the newest player for the Houston Rockets. Hakeem Olajuwon and another rookie, Michael Jordan, excited many fans that year.

During the 1993–94 season, the Houston Rockets won the NBA championship. In 1994, Olajuwon became the only player in the history of the NBA to be named the league's regular season Most Valuable Player (MVP), Defensive Player of the Year, and MVP during the finals in one season.

Olajuwon had been raised as a Muslim, but when he first arrived in America he didn't practice his religion. After college, though, Olajuwon rediscovered Islam. He made a commitment to put his religion first. This worried his coaches and fans in 1995 when the holy month of Ramadan fell during the basketball season. Olajuwon observed the daily fasts even though he had difficulty playing. Ramadan ended before the playoffs, however, and Olajuwon made a tremendous comeback. The Rockets won the NBA championship for the second year in a row. Olajuwon was once again named MVP in the finals, the only center in history to receive the award two years in a row.

In 1996, Olajuwon played for the U.S. men's basketball team in the Summer Olympics. (He became eligible to play for the United States in 1993, when he became a U.S. citizen.)

He retired from basketball in 2002.

*Houston Rockets' seven-foot-tall center, Hakeem Olajuwon, dunks the basketball and scores two points for his team.*

# Life in America

## Family

Americans generally consider their immediate family—parents and children—to be their family. "Mother" and "father" are names used only for the two parents who raise an individual. In Nigeria, the concept of family is much more expansive. Children often call all the adults in their extended family "Mama" or "Papa" and are expected to obey them. While rural Nigerians may include all distant relatives in their village when speaking of family, those who live in urban areas describe their family in more Westernized terms.

In traditional Nigerian societies, men are the unquestioned head of the family. Their first loyalty is to their mother, rather than their wife. This can create misunderstandings or resentment when men from traditional backgrounds marry women who were raised in America. Arranged marriages are still commonplace among Nigerian immigrant families, but the couple generally has the final approval.

The emphasis on equality for men and women in America has affected most Nigerian families in some way, especially those who were raised in rural areas. Parents who were raised in Nigeria tend to accept traditional roles for men and women. That is, men are expected to earn the income, provide food and housing, and make all the important decisions for the family. Women are expected to care for the children and home. While many women also earn income, both in Nigeria and in America, this income doesn't always give them a say in household decisions. Some families have adopted an American-style approach, with both men and women helping with household chores and making decisions together. Other families maintain traditional roles within the family and adopt American values as needed in their professional lives.

Women often experience the most conflict about the differing roles and expectations in America and Nigeria, especially when they are raising daughters. While many Nigerian women welcome the greater independence and equality that

**Did you know?**

In some ethnic groups, such as the Igbo, women traditionally cannot buy land or conduct other business transactions; a male family member must represent them.

American women enjoy, they also worry that they are not raising their daughters to follow Igbo, Yoruba, or other ethnic group traditions. They are proud of their daughters when they excel in academics, but worry that the girls' successes will cause them to be ostracized by traditional Nigerians.

Feeling caught between two widely differing cultures, the women often compromise by reminding their daughters about traditional behavior (wearing dresses, speaking softly) and accepting their "American" conduct (wearing pants and shorts, speaking up for themselves). Churches and community organizations support parents' efforts to provide a strong cultural heritage for their children by conducting naming and rite-of-passage ceremonies and other traditional rituals.

Nigerian men do not face the same problems as women when they immigrate to America. The same qualities that are valued in America–independence, assertiveness, and competitiveness–are also valued qualities for Nigerian men.

## Work

Most of the Nigerians in America, both men and women, are well educated and speak fluent English. Many attended schools in the United States before becoming permanent residents. Although many Nigerians are professionals, they may have to work in other fields when they first arrive in the United States, due to licensing requirements.

## What's in a Name?

Nigerian American communities strengthen their cultural heritage by continuing to observe traditional rituals in America. For the Yoruba people, the naming ceremony is one of the most important rituals in an individual's life. In Nigeria, the ceremony is usually performed when a baby is seven to nine days old. But in America, the baby may be several months old at the time of the ceremony if the family chooses to wait until grandparents or other family members in Nigeria can attend.

The naming ceremony usually takes place in the family's home in America. In Nigeria, it is often held outdoors. The family's pastor conducts the ceremony, which often combines Christian practices with traditional Yoruba rituals. A table holds foods and objects that are important to the ceremony. The pastor introduces each item to the baby, encouraging the child to touch or taste it. The Yoruba believe that introducing these symbolic materials at an early age will help children grow up to become well-respected, contributing members of the community.

# School

The experiences of Nigerian children in American schools vary widely based on whether they were raised in rural or urban areas, north or south. Although most young immigrant children have attended a primary school where classes are conducted in English, access to Western-style secondary schools varies from region to region. In the south, the education system is modeled on British and American school systems. Classes are conducted in English and cover many of the same subjects as in American schools. Students in rural areas are more likely to participate in apprenticeship programs, while northern schools teach math, science, and language in an Islamic environment. (The Nigerian government prohibited private and church-owned schools from the mid-1970s until 1990.)

Handling insulting and ignorant questions and comments from their American peers is a top complaint of many immigrant children. Many American students assume that all Africans know each other, sleep in trees, don't wear clothing, and see lions everywhere. Students from Nigeria often have to adjust to the more assertive attitudes and expectations in American schools. Some have to make a special effort to look adults in the eye or to speak up for themselves, actions that may have been considered ill-mannered where they were raised but that are rewarded in American classrooms.

Parents also have to make adjustments as they interact with teachers and school officials. Work schedules may not allow parents to attend all the parent-teacher events and conferences. Some community organizations encourage parents to build on Nigerian tradition and form parent groups that share responsibility for checking on each other's children.

The lack of discipline in American schools as compared to schools in Nigeria concerns many parents. They also worry that their children may have difficulty defining who they are as Nigerians in America. For these reasons, some parents send their American-born children to stay with family members and attend school in Nigeria.

A large number of Nigerian and Nigerian American students graduate from colleges and universities in America. They generally choose professions such as information technology, medicine, law, and education.

# Religion

Most of the Nigerians who have immigrated to America are Christians. They are about equally divided between Roman Catholics and Protestants. In America, Protestants often attend independent churches that are branches of independent Nigerian churches, which were established in protest against the policies of major denominations. In some denominations, Nigerians were not allowed to become clergy, or pastors. Other Western denominations wouldn't allow traditional customs to be part of the worship service.

*Nigerian-born Chief Amoo Tony Ogunsusi conducts a libation ceremony to bless the new museum for the African/African American Historical Society of Allen County/ Northeast Indiana in Fort Wayne on February 1, 2000. The libation ceremony blends traditional African and Christian rituals.*

Both independent and Catholic churches in America offer support to immigrants in their congregations. Church members help newly arrived Nigerians find work and a place to live. They also provide emotional and financial support as the new immigrants get used to life in America.

## Holidays and Festivals

As Christians, Nigerians celebrate the same holidays as most Americans. Families often schedule an extended trip home to Nigeria for Christmas. The extra time at the holidays gives them an opportunity to visit with family and friends whom they haven't seen for months. Nigerians living in America are expected to bring gifts for all their family members and friends when they return for a visit.

## The Arts

Music is an integral part of day-to-day life in Nigeria. Some musical forms, mostly vocal music accompanied by traditional instruments such as drums and bells, are traditional to a specific ethnic group. Other music combines traditional rhythms with the instruments or music of other cultures to produce a completely new sound. Afrobeat music, one of the best known of Nigeria's musical forms, is one such combination. It mixes drumming and vocal elements from traditional Yoruba music with jazz, funk, and big-band sounds. *Juju* music, another well-known Nigerian musical style, emerged as an alternative to the highlife music enjoyed by the upper class. While highlife music is primarily dance music, *juju* combines the traditional Yoruba talking drums with guitars, keyboards, and, sometimes, the accordion. The lyrics usually address social or cultural issues. Afrobeat and *juju* were popular in Europe and America in the 1970s and 1980s.

Among the Igbo in America today, however, Stephen Osita Osadebe reigns supreme. A highlife musician in the traditional vein, he performed in the United States for the first time in 1995, when he was almost 60. Because he is so highly regarded by the Igbo, he plays only private shows. Igbo in Houston or Los Angeles or some other city rent a performance hall for Osadebe's concert. They don't have to worry about advertising—word spreads throughout the community and Igbo immigrants fill the concert halls. In 1995, Osadebe recorded an internationally acclaimed album entitled *Kedu America* (Greetings from America) while on tour in the United States.

## Food

Many of the foods served in traditional Nigerian meals are familiar to Americans, brought across the Atlantic by slaves hundreds of years ago. For instance, the gumbos of the American South have their roots in the seafood soups and stews of the West African coastal regions.

Fresh fruits and vegetables are plentiful and are served at every meal. Yams, cassava, plantain, okra, tomatoes, and hot peppers are the basis of many Nigerian dishes. Oranges, tangerines, bananas, mangoes, guavas, pineapple, pawpaw, coconut, and papaya are also served. Meat is rather expensive, so it is reserved for special occasions or added sparingly to stews. Goat, beef, poultry, fish, and shellfish are all served in Nigerian homes. The only dietary restriction on meat applies to Muslims, whose religion doesn't allow them to eat pork.

In recent years, as the African immigrant community has grown, African food markets have sprung up around Brooklyn, New York, and Washington, D.C. They carry hard-to-find items such as red palm oil, bitter kolas, and yam flour. A farmers' market in the Washington, D.C., area sells mostly African foods, including roasted and smoked goat meat. Given the huge increase in the African population in the Washington area in the last decade and the success of these African markets, it's no surprise that mainstream grocery stores in the area are beginning to carry African foods as well.

*Nigerian shoppers look over the red peppers for sale at a local market in their native country.*

Sharing recipes with family and friends is not always easy for Nigerian women. Traditionally, women learned to cook by watching and helping their mothers. The ability to cook "by instinct" rather than using a recipe was a valued skill. Ingredients and cooking times were rarely measured. Instead, the women used their experience and gut instinct, tasting the dish periodically to adjust spices or cooking time. In America, some Nigerian women are beginning to record their traditional recipes so they will be able to pass them on to their children.

## Jollof Rice

*This dish is often eaten with fried plantains and meat. Sometimes the meat is cooked with the rice.*

4 cups rice

6 cups water

2 tomatoes, quartered

1 bell pepper, seeded

1 onion, finely chopped

1 cup chicken or beef broth

Water

Salt to taste

Cayenne pepper

In a large pot, combine the rice and water. Cook over high heat for 10 to 15 minutes. Place the tomatoes, bell pepper, and, if desired, the onion in a food processor or blender. Process until they are smooth.

After the rice has cooked, add the tomato mixture. If you didn't process the onion with the tomatoes, add it to the pot now. Add the broth and, if necessary, any additional water needed to finish cooking the rice. (It is better to add a little at a time as needed than to add too much water and have a soupy dish.)

Add salt and cayenne pepper to taste. The dish is done when the rice is soft and there is no excess liquid in the pan. If the rice is done before all the liquid evaporates, turn the heat to low and simmer until the rice is dry.

Note: You can substitute 8 ounces of canned tomato sauce and 3 ounces of canned tomato paste for the fresh tomatoes.

Serves 6 to 8.

*Source: Adapted from Motherland Nigeria.com*
*http://motherlandnigeria.com/food.html*

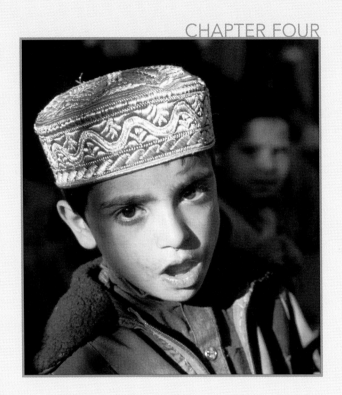

# CHAPTER FOUR

# Pakistanis

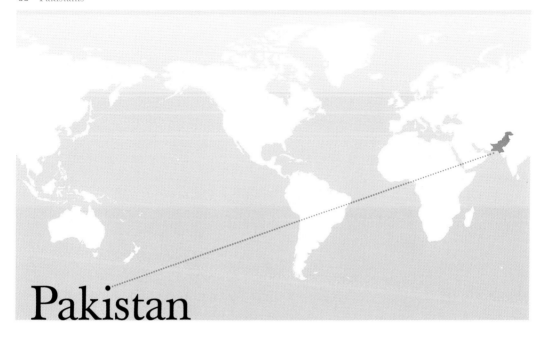

# Pakistan

is a relatively young country in South Asia. Formerly part of India, it became an independent nation in 1947 when the British government relinquished control of its *colony.* Today, Pakistan is an important ally of the United States in the war against terrorism.

Located between Afghanistan and India, Pakistan is home to five major *ethnic groups,* each with its own language. Pakistan's official language is Urdu, a language that combines elements of Hindi, Arabic, and Persian languages. English is widely used in Pakistan as well, especially in government, business, higher education, and the military.

About two-thirds of Pakistan's people are Punjabi (pun-JAH-bee). They live primarily in the northeastern province of Punjab, home to Pakistan's capital city of Islamabad (is-LAH-muh-*bahd*). Besides being the most populous group, Punjabis are among the wealthiest and best-educated Pakistanis. Punjabis are well represented in government and the military.

Sindhis (SIN-dees) live in the southeastern province of Sindh. Once a Hindu province, Sindh today is mostly Muslim. Most Sindhis are very poor. Many are farmers, but they often have to give most of their harvest to the wealthy landowners. They make up about 13 percent of the population.

In the North-West Frontier Province live the Pathans (puh-TAHNS), a fiercely independent tribal group that is known as Pashtun (pash-TOON) in Afghanistan. They are among the most conservative Muslims in Pakistan. About 9 percent of Pakistan's people are Pathan.

Muhajir (muh-HAH-jir) is the name given to Muslim *refugees* who moved from India to Pakistan during the separation of the two countries. They are primarily Urdu-speaking business people living in cities such as Karachi and Islamabad. Although Muhajir families have lived in Pakistan for over fifty years, they are still considered outsiders. They make up about 8 percent of the population.

Balochistan (buh-*loo*-chuh-STAN) Province is home to the Baluchi (buh-LOO-chee) ethnic group, which comprises about 3 percent of the population. The Baluchis live a traditional life for the most part, as nomadic herders who move from place to place to find grazing pastures for their sheep and goats. Modern irrigation and farming methods, along with the discovery of natural gas and mineral deposits, are threatening the Baluchis' way of life.

# A Quick Look Back

Although Pakistan didn't exist as a nation prior to 1947, the history of the region extends back thousands of years. In fact, it was home to one of the world's earliest *civilizations*. Around 2500 B.C., the Indus Valley civilization grew along the Indus River, which stretches from north to south through eastern Pakistan. The people living there established cities, a writing system, and an *economic* system that included trading with Sumer, an ancient civilization in what is now Iraq.

*Archaeologists have uncovered the ruins of the Indus Valley civilization of Mohenjo-Daro near Sindh, Pakistan.*

The religion of Islam was introduced in the region early in the eighth century. The first Muslim community was established in the Sindh Province. From there, Islamic influence spread throughout the region.

## British Rule

The British East India Company began trading in India in the early 1600s. The earliest trading posts were established along the southeastern coast, but the British gradually expanded throughout India. Uprisings against the British in 1857 led the British government to take over control of India from the East India Company.

## A New Nation

With Hindus in the majority in India, Muslim leaders worried that the British government would not be responsive to their concerns. When political parties were allowed in the 1880s, Muslims joined with Hindus to create the Indian National Congress, a group that promoted independence from Britain. Later, the Muslims broke away to form the Muslim League.

The growing independence movement put pressure on the British government to make changes. Increasing animosity between the Hindu and Muslim factions seemed likely to develop into a civil war if drastic changes weren't made. Unwilling to send more troops to keep the peace, the British began planning for India's independence after World War II (1939–1945). Muslim leader Muhammad Ali Jinnah pushed for the creation of an independent Muslim state. On August 14, 1947, Pakistan became an independent country within the British Commonwealth. India gained its independence the next day.

### Pakistan

The name "Pakistan" means "the land of the pure" in Urdu, its official language.

At independence, Pakistan was divided into two sections: West Pakistan, which encompasses present-day Pakistan, and East Pakistan, which is now the country of Bangladesh. In between was India. As a result of the division, millions of Muslims in India migrated to Pakistan, while millions of Hindus and Sikhs in Pakistan migrated to India. Violence and bloodshed accompanied these migrations. Over 1 million Muslims and Hindus were killed as they tried to move from one country to another.

Although Muslims had achieved their goal of a separate nation, they faced many difficulties. The government, economic structure, and educational system had to be developed from the ground up. Muhammad Ali Jinnah, the well-respected and much loved founder of Pakistan, became the first governor-general of the country, but he died after a year in office. With 1,000 miles (1,600 kilometers) and different languages dividing East and West Pakistan, tensions grew. East Pakistan wanted to govern itself locally while sharing foreign policy and defense with West Pakistan. West Pakistan wanted one unified nation.

*A Pakistani soldier looks at the destruction from Indian shelling at the Abkar military post northeast of Islamabad.*

## Kashmir

The state of Jammu and Kashmir, commonly called Kashmir, links India and Pakistan at their northern borders. Since the time of partition, India and Pakistan have both claimed Kashmir.

The conflict began in 1947 when the ruler of Kashmir, who was Hindu, was deciding whether to affiliate Kashmir with India or Pakistan. Pakistanis thought Kashmir should be made part of their country because most of the people who lived there were Muslim. In an effort to force a decision, the Pakistani army invaded Kashmir, where it fought a battle with the Indian army. At the end of the two-year dispute, Kashmir was divided, with most of the state going to India.

In 1956, the Pakistani *constitution* was rewritten, making Pakistan an Islamic republic. This meant that Islam became the official religion of the nation. However, Pakistan's legal system continued to be based on the British system. The new constitution also created a new legislature that was split evenly between East and West Pakistan. The instability in the government continued, however, and in 1958, martial law was declared. (Under martial law, the military, rather than elected or civilian leaders, rules the country.) General Muhammad Ayub Khan (muh-HAM-id AH-yoob kahn) proceeded to rule Pakistan for over ten years.

Following the Kashmir war of 1965, Ayub lost the support of many Pakistanis. By 1969, he declared martial law once again and selected General Agha Muhammad Yahya Khan as president. After a few months in office, Yahya announced a return to a constitutional government, with elections to be held in 1970. He also declared that representation in the National Assembly would be based on the population of each province, rather than the earlier constitutional directive that gave equal representation to East and West Pakistan.

These changes gave East Pakistan a strong majority in the legislature. As a result, the West Pakistani legislators, led by Zulfikar Ali Bhutto, stated that they would not attend the legislative session, making it impossible to return to a civilian government. In 1971, Yahya postponed the National Assembly indefinitely. Strikes and protests erupted immediately in East Pakistan. Within a month, East Pakistan announced its independence from Pakistan.

Civil war broke out between East and West Pakistan following the declaration of independence. After about nine months of fighting, India joined the battle, fighting on the side of East Pakistan. Within days, the war was over and East Pakistan became the independent country of Bangladesh.

## Changes in Pakistan

Yahya was severely criticized for the loss of East Pakistan. He resigned and turned control of the government over to Zulfikar Ali Bhutto. Under Bhutto's leadership, much needed social institutions such as schools and hospitals were strengthened. The army's control over government policy was limited. And a new constitution was drafted. When elections were held in 1973, Bhutto was elected prime minister, the most powerful government official in Pakistan.

Although Bhutto had instituted many reforms, he faced opposition from wealthy Pakistanis because the reforms diluted their control over the economy and government. Religious leaders considered many of the reforms un-Islamic. After winning the 1977 elections, Bhutto was accused of election fraud by the opposition. After several weeks of protests, Bhutto was overthrown in a *coup* led by General Muhammad Zia ul-Haq (muh-HAM-id ZEE-ah ool-HAHK). Two years later Bhutto was executed.

At the time of the coup, General Zia announced plans to hold elections within three months. However, he cancelled the election plans and soon began ruling as a dictator. Freedom of the press was curtailed and people who spoke out against Zia's policies were often imprisoned. Political parties were banned. In 1978, Zia announced that Pakistan's laws would be compared to Islamic law. Any laws that did not conform to Islamic principles would be abolished. Zia also began developing nuclear weapons. In 1988, Zia finally decided to allow elections. Before they could be held, however, he died in a suspicious plane crash.

## Changing Leadership

In 1988, Benazir Bhutto (*ben*-uh-ZIR BOOT-toh), daughter of Zulfikar Ali Bhutto, became the first woman to lead an Islamic nation. As leader of the political party founded by her father, Bhutto automatically became prime minister when that party won the most legislative seats in the election. However, she was removed from power two years later amidst charges that her government was corrupt.

Nawaz Sharif replaced Bhutto as prime minister in 1990. He moved quickly to make Islamic law, or Shari'a, the basis of all Pakistani law. Shari'a became more important than the constitution in deciding the outcome of court cases. President Ishaq Khan and Sharif frequently clashed on government policy. When their individual struggles for power finally brought the country to an impasse in 1993, they both were forced to resign their offices.

Benazir Bhutto became prime minister once more following the 1993 elections.

Nawar Sharif became prime minister when Bhutto failed to retain her power, following the 1997 elections. During

Sharif's second term, tensions between ethnic and religious groups in Pakistan increased, especially in the Sindh Province. The ongoing dispute over Kashmir also intensified. Pakistan was declared to be in a state of emergency following nuclear weapons testing by both India and Pakistan in 1998. The United States and others in the international community placed economic *sanctions* on both countries for the nuclear tests.

Sharif faced growing criticism over his handling of the Kashmir conflict. General Pervez Musharraf (pur-VAHS moo-SHAR-uhf), head of the Pakistan army at the time, overthrew Sharif's government in 1999. Musharraf's priority was improving Pakistan's economy, but he soon found that the international community doesn't provide loans or aid to military governments.

*President General Pervez Musharraf addresses his country's troops at an undisclosed forward position near the Pakistani border with India in May 2002.*

## Pakistan Today

The dispute over Kashmir's future continues to occupy India and Pakistan. By the start of 2002, the two countries had posted about 1 million troops along the Kashmir-Pakistan border. Later that year, however, both sides began withdrawing troops from the border following diplomatic efforts by the international community. However, threats of nuclear attacks from both Pakistan and India in 2003 raised the possibility of war once more.

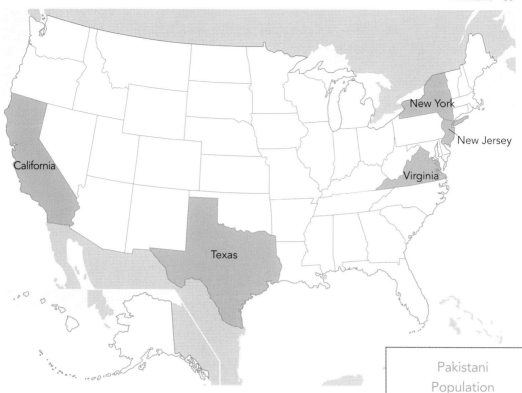

| Pakistani Population in the U.S. | |
| --- | --- |
| New York | 34,039 |
| California | 26,348 |
| Texas | 20,206 |
| New Jersey | 14,620 |
| Virginia | 11,534 |

*Source: U.S. Census, 2000*

# Coming to America

When Pakistan became an independent nation in 1947, the United States had very restrictive quotas on immigration, so few people *immigrated*. The 1960 census showed fewer than 2,000 people of Pakistani descent living in America. After the quotas were lifted in 1965, however, immigration from Pakistan rapidly increased, doubling each decade through the 1990s. By 2000, over 265,000 U.S. residents reported that they had been born in Pakistan.

These *immigrants* were, for the most part, highly educated professionals who were looking for economic opportunities and increased stability for their children. Pakistanis settled in urban areas across the United States. The biggest communities, however, formed in major cities such as New York City, Chicago, and Washington, D.C.

U.S./Pakistani Immigration by Decade

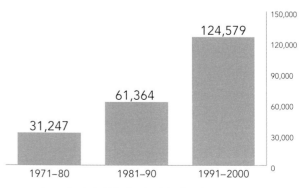

| | | |
| --- | --- | --- |
| 1971–80 | 1981–90 | 1991–2000 |
| 31,247 | 61,364 | 124,579 |

*Source:* Statistical Yearbook of the Immigration and Naturalization Service

The Immigration and Naturalization Service estimates that 41,000 Pakistanis were living in the United States illegally in 1996, the fifteenth largest group of illegal immigrants.

# Life in America

Although Pakistani immigrants come from a country whose major religion and values are very different from those they encounter in America, they are among the most successful immigrants in the United States. With experience in multiparty governments, they are the most politically active immigrants in America. While there are many socially oriented Pakistani American organizations in the United States, many groups have formed for the purpose of lobbying America's Congress on issues of concern to Pakistan.

### *Spotlight on*
### SAGHIR TAHIR

In 2000, Saghir Tahir became the first Muslim elected to the New Hampshire State Assembly. He also has the distinction of holding the highest elected office of any Pakistani American.

A civil engineer by trade, Tahir immigrated to the United States in 1972. Six years later he became an American citizen. As a specialist in roofing and waterproofing, Tahir often testifies as an expert witness in court cases.

After the 2001 terrorist attacks in the United States, Tahir received many calls from family and friends in Pakistan. They worried that Muslims, and Pakistanis in particular, were not being treated fairly in America. In response, Tahir led a team of eight naturalized Pakistani Americans to visit Pakistan. The delegation's purpose was to share their positive view of America with Pakistanis. They wanted to assure people in their homeland that America provided freedom of religion, tolerance, human rights, and a good life.

In sharing his message, Tahir said, "We are successful because Pakistan gave us the tools and America gave us the opportunity. We owe people from both countries a great deal."

## Family

Like many immigrant families, Pakistanis are very close. In both America and Pakistan, extended family members may share a household. Predominantly Muslim, the new immigrants work hard to maintain their values and traditions as they adopt some American customs. In families that are able to live on one salary, the wife stays home to care for the children. Men usually help with chores outside of the house. They may also help take care of the children.

For many Pakistanis, life in America means access to much more technology than is affordable in their homeland. Dishwashers, microwaves, vacuums, and other household appliances are available in Pakistan, but they are very expensive and few people own them.

*This Pakistani family was photographed shortly after they immigrated to Chicago, Illinois, in 1992.*

Pakistani children growing up in America often have difficulty determining where they fit in. They often feel different from other Americans because of their name or religion or clothing. Yet, because they were born in or grew up in America, they are not considered Pakistani by relatives in Pakistan. As the Pakistani community in America has grown over the years, organizations have formed that offer young people an opportunity to socialize with peers who share many of the same concerns.

## Work

The majority of Pakistani immigrants—men and women—are highly educated professionals. They work as scientists, computer programmers, engineers, doctors, and business people. Many are entrepreneurs, opening electronics stores and life insurance companies, restaurants and video stores in America.

In New York City, many Pakistanis have found work driving taxicabs. By 1997, about half of all cabdrivers in New York City were from Pakistan, India, or Bangladesh, an increase of over 700 percent since 1984. Mostly men, these immigrants work long hours for relatively low pay. Because they have to lease the cab, some immigrants form partnerships, which allow the cab to be driven twenty-four hours a day. The Pakistani drivers have faced prejudice from passengers as well as from other drivers.

In Chicago, another American city with a large Pakistani population, South Asian immigrants, including Pakistanis, dominate the doughnut industry. In the 1970s, an immigrant from India found success by opening and managing doughnut shops in the Chicago area. He shared his expertise with other immigrants from South Asia, encouraging them to open doughnut shops as well. By 1999, Indian and Pakistani immigrants owned about 90 percent of all the Dunkin' Donuts stores in Chicago and the surrounding areas.

The success of these businesses is attributed to family loyalty and a supportive immigrant community. Many of the businesses are family-owned, so they have a dependable low-cost labor source. The immigrant community also stands ready to help as needed, from offering advice on running the shop efficiently to stepping in to run the shop in case of an emergency.

## Spotlight on
### SAFIA KHALIL

Safia Khalil never dreamed that she would accomplish all that she has so far. Growing up in Karachi, Pakistan, she never went anywhere on her own. Except for visits to relatives in India, she never left Karachi. Her life changed tremendously, however, when Khalil followed through on her university professors' suggestions to apply for postgraduate work in the United States. She was accepted at the University of Oklahoma. She then had to convince her parents to let her go.

Today, Khalil analyzes human genome data as a member of a cancer research team for a pharmaceutical company. In her spare time, she works to create the Pakistani Women's Computing Initiative. This project is founded on the idea that computers will give women in Pakistan an opportunity to gain more control over their lives. Khalil and her cofounder, Arifa Khandwalla, hope to convince American corporations to donate computers to the project. They are currently seeking funding to pay for instructors who will train Pakistani women in using the computers.

# School

Pakistani parents recognize the importance of a good education for their children. They encourage both their sons and daughters to take advantage of all the opportunities that America offers in this regard. Although English is not an official language in Pakistan, it is widely used. Most Pakistani children, therefore, have some knowledge of English when they arrive in the United States. Schools with large populations of Pakistani students often offer bilingual classes in English and Urdu.

One of the hardest things for students, especially teenagers, to deal with at school is the wide divergence between Muslim and American values. Parents try to bridge these differences by helping in classrooms, introducing Pakistani foods and Muslim traditions to their children's classmates. Parents have also lobbied school boards for recognition of major Islamic holidays and values. As a result, many school districts are more sympathetic to their Muslim students' restrictions. Changes include such things as segregating physical education classes by gender.

# Religion

About 97 percent of Pakistanis in Pakistan are Muslim. By far the largest group are Sunni Muslims (77 percent), while 20 percent are Shiite. Only 3 percent of Pakistanis follow Christianity, Hinduism, or other religions. (To learn more about the religion of Islam, see pages 33–34 of *The Newest Americans*, Volume 1.)

In the large urban areas of the United States, mosques are relatively easy to find. In rural America, however, Pakistani Muslims may have to drive two hours to reach a mosque for Friday prayers.

School children are often asked how they spent Christmas vacation or what presents they received for Christmas. Since Muslims don't celebrate Christmas, it is often an awkward time for kids.

**Did you know?**

Many Muslim children fast for the first time at age seven. By the time they are fourteen, they are usually fasting for the whole month of Ramadan. In Pakistan, younger children often keep a *chiri roza*, or bird fast, to help them feel included in Ramadan. During *chiri roza*, children fast from breakfast until lunch and from lunch until *iftar* (dinner).

# Holidays and Festivals

Most of the holidays celebrated in Pakistan are religious in nature. This tradition continues in America, where the holidays allow the Pakistani American community to gather and celebrate together.

Pakistani American organizations often host *iftar* parties during the month of Ramadan. During Ramadan, devout Muslims do not eat or drink anything from sunrise to sunset. When the sun sets, prayers are said and the family gathers for *iftar*–a meal to break the fast. The Pakistani American *iftar* parties encourage family and friends to socialize by breaking the fast together.

Eid al-Fitr and Eid al-Adha are joyous occasions. Gifts are exchanged between family and friends, and there is a wonderful feast. Community groups often sponsor Eid celebrations as well as Chand Raat bazaars. Held the evening before Eid, Chand Raat offers Pakistani immigrants an opportunity to purchase gifts and food for the next day's celebration. Using the art called *mehndi,* women and children may have their hands painted in intricate designs using henna, a reddish brown dye.

*Dipali Shah of Randolph, Massachusetts, paints the hand of a Worcester State College student using a method called* mehndi *at the India Day Festival held on the college campus.*

Pakistani Americans also gather for nonreligious celebrations and festivals. One of the most colorful is Basant, a kite-flying festival held in the spring. People gather in parks or fields to fly kites of all sizes and shapes. Kite-fighting competitions are a popular part of Basant festivals. Participants coat the strings of their kites with crushed glass and then maneuver their kites in an effort to cut the strings of their competitors' kites. The person with the last kite flying is the winner.

Pakistan's Independence Day is also celebrated by Pakistani Americans. While August 14 is the official Independence Day, it may be celebrated on the nearest weekend in America. The community may gather for a picnic or for a formal banquet that features speeches and Pakistani music and dance.

Although Pakistani Muslims don't celebrate Christmas, December 25 is a special day to all Pakistanis—it is the birthday of Muhammad Ali Jinnah, the founder of Pakistan.

## The Arts

Music has always played an important role in Pakistani culture. *Qawwali,* music that is considered a method of worship by many Muslims, has long been supported by the government. Drums and handclapping provide the rhythm, while the melody is played on a harmonium (a small, hand-pumped organ). The lyrics of each song come from Islamic mystical poems. In the 1970s, *qawwali* music made its debut in the West with a performance at Carnegie Hall in New York City. One of the most successful *qawwali* musicians was Nusrat Fateh Ali Khan. His musical talents were admired by American musicians and film producers, who used his compositions in the soundtracks of American films. In turn, Ali Khan incorporated Western instruments and sounds into his music.

American Pakistani communities often invite Pakistani musicians to play at their events and celebrations.

## Food

Pakistani food has much in common with that of its neighbors—India, Afghanistan, and Iran. Spices such as cinnamon, cardamom, cloves, black mustard seeds, coriander, and saffron add a rich and complex flavor to the dishes. Peppers are often added as well, making the dish hot and spicy.

A typical Pakistani meal includes a curry of meat and vegetables served with rice. Flat bread, called chapati or roti, is often served with the curry. Tea, or *chai* (*cheye*), is a favorite drink throughout Pakistan. It is usually very sweet, with milk added.

## Fruit Chaat (Spicy Fruit Salad)

2 apples, cored and cut into bite-sized chunks

2 pears, cored and cut into bite-sized chunks

2 oranges, peeled and cut into bite-sized chunks

3/4 cup fresh pomegranate seeds

1 cup white seedless grapes, halved

1 cup red seedless grapes, halved

1 big mango, peeled and cut into bite-sized chunks

3 bananas, peeled and sliced

2 teaspoons salt

1/4 cup sugar

3/4 teaspoon chili powder

2 teaspoons *chaat masala* (see recipe at right)

juice of 2 lemons

juice of 2 oranges

Combine the prepared fruits in a large bowl. Sprinkle with the salt, sugar, chili powder, and *chaat masala*. Pour the lemon and orange juice over the ingredients. Mix well, then cover and chill slightly before serving.

## Chaat Masala (Seasoning Mix)

2 tablespoons cumin seeds

1 tablespoon coriander seeds

1 tablespoon aniseed

1 1/2 teaspoons freshly ground black pepper

1 1/2 teaspoons dry ginger

1 1/2 teaspoons red chili powder

1 1/2 teaspoons ground lemon salt

1 1/2 teaspoons ground black salt (*kala namak*)

1/2 teaspoon table salt

Grind cumin, coriander, and aniseed in a small electric mill or food processor. (Seeds may be roasted first, if desired.) Mix with remaining ingredients. Store in an airtight container.

*Source: Cooking with BJ: Pakistani Cookery*
*http://www.contactpakistan.com/pakfood/snack/fruitchaat.htm*

# CHAPTER FIVE

# Poles

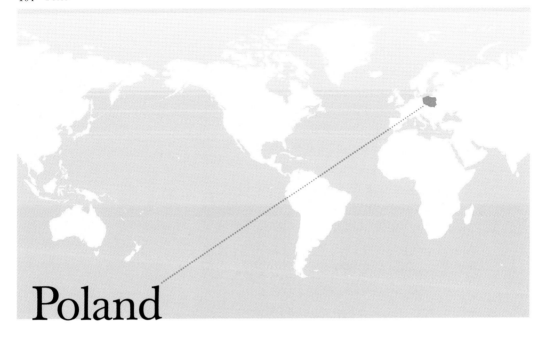

# Poland

is the ninth largest country in Europe, slightly bigger than Italy. One *ethnic group,* the Poles, makes up nearly 98 percent of Poland's population. Because of its expanding and shrinking borders during its long history, a small percentage of the population is German, Ukrainian, and Belarusian.

## A Quick Look Back

Poland was founded in A.D. 966 by Slavonic tribes who had been living in the region for thousands of years. They developed ties with neighboring Bohemia as protection against invasions from Germanic tribes in the west. By 1109, Poland claimed the land from the Baltic to the Black Sea. When it united with Lithuania in the fifteenth century, Poland became the largest country in Europe.

The nation was weakened by internal strife in the seventeenth century. By the end of the eighteenth century, agreements between Poland's powerful neighbors divided the country among Russia, Prussia (now Germany), and Austria. Poland had disappeared from the face of Europe.

Poland did not reappear as an independent country until after World War I

### Poland

It is amazing that Poland appears on the map of Europe at all. In its long and embattled history, it has been totally absorbed by other countries twice.

(1914–1918). On June 28, 1919, the Treaty of Versailles (ver-SIGH) spelled out the terms of Germany's surrender to the Allied forces. The Germans were humiliated by the concessions they had to agree to. As a part of the treaty, the Polish territory that the Germans had occupied between 1772 and 1919 was returned to make Poland independent once more.

The new *regime* got off to a shaky start and in 1926, after fourteen coalition governments, the military seized control in a *coup*. Josef Pilsudski (yoh-sef PILL-sud-skee), a Polish war hero, took power as the leader of the coup. He governed in a strict, authoritarian style until his death in 1935.

## Polani

The name of the country, Poland, comes from the word Polani (PO-lah-knee), which means "people of the fields." That was the name given to the loose group of tribes that originally settled on the Vistula River. The Poles are from one ethnic group. They are almost all Slavs, and they speak the same language with a few regional differences.

## World War II

Adolf Hitler, the leader of Nazi Germany, had the humiliation of the Treaty of Versailles in mind in 1939 when he demanded that Poland turn over control of the city of Gdansk (geh-DONSHK) to Germany. The city, once known as Danzig, had been part of the German-occupied Polish territory until 1919. Poland refused and World War II (1939–1945) soon began.

Warsaw, the capital of Poland, was bombed by the German air force on the morning of September 1, 1939. On September 17, the Soviets invaded Poland from the east. The Russians wanted to expand their territory and saw the German move into Poland as their opportunity. Even though Britain and France had promised to support Poland if it was overrun, the promise was not honored when the Germans and Russians invaded Poland.

After fierce fighting, the Soviet Union and Germany agreed to divide Poland's land between them. This was the beginning of a dark time for Poland. Hitler began moving Poles off land that it had seized. The Russians imprisoned 2 million Poles who had resisted the Soviet takeover. These people were tortured and sent to prison camps in Siberia or the Russian Arctic.

A Polish resistance movement was formed as well as a government-in-exile in Paris, France. When France fell to Germany also, the Polish government was moved to London, England. Inside Poland, an underground Polish Home Army fought a *guerrilla* war against the Germans. Over 500,000 Poles participated. They destroyed bridges, disrupted German communications, and blew up German war equipment.

## Under Communism

After five-and-a-half years of war, the Allies finally conquered Nazi Germany on May 8, 1945. At the war's end, Poland had lost over 6.5 million people, Warsaw lay in ruins, and the Polish people were starving. The European map was redrawn once more. Poland lost much of its land to the Soviet Union, but regained territory from the fallen Germany. The Soviet Union moved in to take control of Poland, unchallenged by the other war-weary Allies—including the United States and Great Britain. A "people's republic" was formed in which the Communist Party held all control.

## Solidarity

The Soviets tried to win Polish acceptance by providing social services, inexpensive food, and free education. But increasing economic problems and unhappiness over a lack of freedom caused riots, with Polish workers shouting, "No bread without freedom."

In 1980, a coalition of workers formed Solidarnosc (SOL-i-DAR-i-nosht), or Solidarity, and a grassroots political movement began. With 10 million members in 1981, Solidarity became the first trade union in a Communist-controlled country to operate independently of the Soviets. Its freedom was short-lived, though. In December of that year, martial law was declared. Six thousand members of the union were arrested, including Solidarity's leader, Lech Walesa (lek VAH-len-sah).

In 1989, as a result of continued pressure by the United States and other countries, the Communist leadership of Poland once again recognized Solidarity as a legal entity, gave legal rights to the church and the press, and adopted a new *constitution*. Poland's first free elections were held in

### Solidarnosc

In Gdansk in December of 1970, Polish workers were killed outside the gates of the Lenin Shipyard while protesting the enormous price increases by the Communist regime. Soviet tanks were sent to stop 10,000 Polish protesters. On that same site in 1980, Lech Walesa was elected by Solidarity to be the new labor union's leader. Solidarity rapidly became the movement that Polish resistance politics centered around.

June of that same year. Solidarity won all but one of the *Senat* (sen-AHD) seats and all of the *Sejm* (SAME) seats that it was permitted to contest. A non-Communist government was formed with Tadeusz Mazowiecki (TAH-doos MAH-so-veesh-kee) as prime minister and General Wojciech Jaruzelski (yah-ROOZ-el-skee) as president.

## Lech Walesa

Lech Walesa was born in 1943 and grew up in a small village in Poland. He loved school and debate from an early age, but his parents could not afford to send him to college. Instead he became a skilled worker who found a job in the huge Lenin Shipyard in Gdansk. Walesa and his family and friends would listen to Radio Free Europe and talk politics in the evenings.

The failing Polish economy caused shipyard workers to be given less work and less money. New price increases for goods and services came just before Christmas 1970. Walesa joined his fellow workers up and down the Baltic coast in strikes. He began to give speeches to rally his fellow workers and argued with his employers about working conditions and pay rates. In 1980, a general strike began and Walesa was able to negotiate a settlement that won freedom for the fledgling trade union.

In 1983, after years of political struggle, fear for his and his family's lives, arrest, and imprisonment, Walesa was awarded the Nobel Peace Prize for his battle for Polish freedom. In 1989, he led the way in achieving the first non-Communist government in Poland in forty years. In 1990, he became president of Poland. Although he was not reelected in the 1995 or 2000 presidential elections, Lech Walesa remains active in Polish politics.

*Supporters carry Polish labor leader Lech Walesa on their shoulders outside the Supreme Court in Warsaw, Poland, on February 10, 1981.*

World opinion and the tide of opinion within Poland forced the weakening Soviet Union to recognize the new Polish government. However, the Polish republic faced many economic and political challenges. Inflation, poor productivity, and poor investment added to the country's mounting troubles. Food prices alone had risen 600 percent. The Mazowiecki government stepped down in 1990, unable to deal with the economic problems. That same year, Solidarity's leader, Lech Walesa, became the new president and eventually Jan Olszewski (yahn owl-CHOOF-skee) was named prime minister of the new cabinet of the Republic of Poland. The two leaders began a policy of strict economic reform as the former Communist country tried to change to a free market economy.

## Poland Today

The young democracy has been troubled by the multitude of political parties that formed in the wake of newfound freedom, making it difficult for any one group to gain a majority of votes on any issue. However, the program of economic responsibility adopted during the early 1990s has enabled Poland to transform its economy into one of the healthiest in Central Europe, boosting the country's hopes of acceptance into the European Union. Poland joined the North Atlantic Treaty Organization (NATO) alliance in 1999.

*A young Polish girl wears a furry green coat, scarf, and furry hat to keep her warm outdoors in the harsh Polish winter.*

Michigan

New York

Pennsylvania

New Jersey

Illinois

## Coming to America

P olish immigrants have been living in the United States since before the American colonies joined together formally in the eighteenth century. Many Polish noblemen, driven out of Poland by the Russians, Prussians (Germans), and Austrians, joined the cause of the American colonies and fought in the Revolution against British rule. However, the greatest Polish migration to America took place in the nineteenth and early twentieth centuries.

The majority of Poles made their way to the big industrial cities like New York City; Pittsburgh, Pennsylvania; Detroit, Michigan; Chicago, Illinois; and Milwaukee, Wisconsin.

Many Polish immigrants tried to re-create their Polish neighborhoods back home. They continued to speak Polish, and even the street signs were written in Polish. They

| Polish Population in the U.S. | |
|---|---|
| Illinois | 725,640 |
| New York | 675,702 |
| Michigan | 665,026 |
| Pennsylvania | 586,110 |
| New Jersey | 408,363 |

*Source: U.S. Census, 2000*

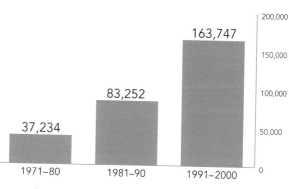

U.S./Polish Immigration by Decade

163,747

83,252

37,234

1971–80     1981–90     1991–2000

*Source:* Statistical Yearbook of the Immigration and Naturalization Service

## Surnames

Many Polish immigrants chose to shorten or change their surnames when they came to America. Americans had difficulty with Polish names because of their lack of vowels and multitude of consonants. Former U.S. senator Edmund Muskie, the Democratic vice-presidential candidate in the 1968 election, was born to Polish immigrant parents in 1914. His Polish name was Edziu Sixtus Marciszewski.

*Senator Edmund S. Muskie (left), Democratic candidate for vice president in 1968, salutes the crowd with his running mate, Vice President Hubert H. Humphrey. Muskie's parents emigrated from Poland and changed their name from Marciszewski to Muskie.*

called themselves *"Polonia."* Regardless of where they settled, they considered themselves an extension of the homeland. Polish Americans often called America the "fourth province of Poland"—the other three being the areas under the control of Russia, Germany, and Austria. The Poles became a small independent society within the larger American sphere, making it easy for them to maintain their Polish heritage and identity.

As first-generation Polish immigrants aged, second- and third-generation Polish Americans fully embraced American culture. These new-generation Polish Americans joined labor unions and political parties and began to lobby for better pay. Education previously had not been that important to the Polish peasants coming to the new country. Now, the children of the peasants began to look to education as a way to move up and into professions and the upper class in American society.

During and after World War II, the United States government passed several acts to allow Polish *refugees,* or displaced persons, entrance into the country. These new World War II immigrants were more educated than their earlier counterparts.

## The 1980s and Beyond

During the Communist regime in Poland after World War II, many intellectuals and Polish *exiles* also made their way to America. In the 1980s and early 1990s, the Polish economy was in a shambles and food shortages were common. Poles longed for freedom from the spying and infiltration into families that the Soviets had instigated. Many Polish immigrants fled to Europe and to the United States. Although some of the *dissidents* who left Poland while it was under Communist rule returned after the 1989 elections, others chose to remain in the United States, where they formed artistic and cultural communities.

Despite changes in Poland today, many Poles still choose to *emigrate* and make their way to the United States. In the year

2000 alone, about 9,800 Polish immigrants came to America. About 5,400 of these were sponsored by family members already in the United States, while 1,400 already had employment secured. Some 2,000 Polish visitors, in the United States on tourist visas, applied for status as permanent residents.

Large Polish communities in Chicago and in neighborhoods like Greenpoint in Brooklyn, New York, still provide a haven for new immigrants. Parts of Greenpoint look like streets in Warsaw or other Polish cities. Employees in groceries speak Polish and street signs are in Polish. Ethnic restaurants feature pickled herring and kielbasa, a Polish sausage. Only Warsaw, the capital of Poland, has more residents of Polish ancestry than Chicago, where over 700,000 claim Polish descent. The existing Polish communities in American cities help newcomers find jobs and adjust slowly to American culture.

## Life in America

Once in America, early Polish immigrants moved into industrial cities where they knew they could find work quickly and form strong communities where they could re-create and foster Polish life and culture.

Challenged by more highly educated Polish immigrants who began to come to the United States during and after World War II, second-, third-, and fourth-generation Polish Americans began to move out from the nest that the early immigrants had built. Seeking higher education and professional jobs, they began to join the wider life of American culture and its diversity outside the neighborhoods.

### Family

Early Polish people referred to their homes as nests, and Polish immigrants brought this image of the home and community to America with them. In America, as in Poland, women were in charge of the household and the children. The man was the authority

### Did you know?

The first Polish people in America arrived at Jamestown, Virginia, in 1608. They were skilled makers of glass, tar, and pitch. These craftspeople set up the first factory in America, a glass works. Later, they built a tar and soap factory.

The Poles in Jamestown also have the distinction of conducting the first strike for equal rights. In 1619, the English colonists were given a voice in the government. The Polish workers were not given representation, and they protested at the first Virginia Assembly. Then they decided to strike. No one else in the colony had the skills to run the factories. So the Poles won their protest and were granted equal rights with the other colonists.

*Chicago's Milwaukee Avenue is considered to be the heart of the city's traditional Polish neighborhood.*

figure. He made the decisions and rules for the family to follow. Children obeyed without question and contributed any money they earned to the household.

By the second and third generation in America, working children no longer wanted to give their paychecks to their fathers. They wanted to save their money for their own future households. The role of the Polish American wife changed as well. Husbands and wives began to make decisions together.

Just as the Polish American family has changed, so have Polish American neighborhoods. They have grown smaller and are often home to other ethnic groups as well. In the 1960s and 1970s, some Polish American neighborhoods were labeled as racist because they resisted desegregation. Many Polish Americans were wary of change and wanted to protect the integrity of their neighborhoods.

Today, many Polish American families have left their ethnic neighborhoods. Many of the younger generation have moved out to the suburbs. Third- and fourth-generation Polish American families have also moved away from many Polish traditions. They marry outside their ethnic group, women work outside the home, and men help with the household chores. Women who do choose to work or do yard work are not seen as "trying to take the man's place." The divorce rate among Polish Americans, however, is still lower than in the general population.

## Work

Although most were farmers in Poland, early Polish immigrant men worked in mines, textile mills, sawmills, and steel and iron factories. They held jobs as blacksmiths, bricklayers, carpenters, tailors, and railroad workers. For people who had worked outside most of their lives, working underground in mines or in hot foundries demanded many personal adjustments and sacrifices.

The mostly uneducated Polish peasants were regarded with prejudice by many Americans, and some employers took advantage of them. Any Pole who spoke broken English became the target of *discrimination*. Although regarded as clever inventors by some company heads, like Henry Ford of the Ford Motor Company, the Poles were often given the hardest and most dangerous jobs. While the best jobs went to white citizens born in America, English, German, Welsh, Scots, and Irish immigrants were given the next best jobs. Then came the Italians, Poles, other Eastern Europeans, and African Americans.

Some early Polish Americans saved their money and opened small businesses like bakeries, butcher shops, grocery stores, saloons, and funeral parlors. The businesses still serve their neighborhoods and give Polish Americans a connection to Polish culture and food. Restaurants and specialty groceries attract people who want apple cake, beet soup, or smoked sausage. From signs posted in the stores, visitors find out about Polish American plays and concerts, or package tours to Poland. Restaurant staff members speak Polish to those wishing to practice their language skills.

Polish immigrants who come to America today are usually very well educated and highly skilled. Many come to America with a corporate job already secured. Of the nearly 3,400 Polish immigrants who came to America in 2000, 38 percent listed their occupation as professional, technical, executive, or managerial. An additional 30 percent described themselves as skilled laborers. With the support of established Polish American communities and good employment prospects, most of these new immigrants make the transition to American culture easily.

## School

Most of the early Polish immigrants came from places in Poland where schools were banned or used to promote the ideas of the invading power. As a result, Poles mistrusted education and educators. Once in America, Polish immigrant children attended Catholic parochial schools until they could work and bring home money for the family. Some Polish American children went to public schools, but under the pressure of the prejudice they felt from other students, many of them dropped out. One second-generation Polish woman recalled, "We all felt scared and embarrassed. We were self-conscious about the way we dressed and the way we looked and spoke. We were a little rough around the edges."

In America today, most Polish Americans want their children to be connected to their proud heritage. Many Polish American communities sponsor Saturday Schools at the local *parish* church. These schools teach Polish American children about Poland's history and the history of Polish Americans in the United States. They also teach Polish language and folklore.

Attitudes about education have changed in the Polish American community. Parents no longer see education as a brainwashing tool of the presiding government as their ancestors did. In the 1950s and 1960s, college was a goal only for the sons of immigrants. Daughters would work and help put the sons through college. But this is an attitude of the past. Polish Americans now work and sacrifice so that their sons and daughters can go to college and achieve a lifestyle higher than their parents'.

Young immigrants from Poland today have a much easier time in school than the early Polish immigrants did. They are sophisticated, educated, and often speak very good English.

## Religion

In America, Polish immigrants continue to be influenced by the Catholic Church. About 95 percent of Polish Americans are Catholic, with about 75 percent practicing. The other 5 percent of Polish Americans are Protestant, Jewish, and Eastern Orthodox.

The Roman Catholic Church has been at the center of life for most Polish Americans. Through their parish, early immigrants with little English could immediately join in picnics, plays, and festivals sponsored by the church and become a part of the life of the community.

Not all established Catholic parishes welcomed Polish immigrants. Most priests did not speak Polish or understand the culture. They made the mistake of trying to make the Poles let go of their culture, learn English quickly, and become Americans. The immigrants, mindful of the autocratic regimes they had escaped, resisted any kind of pressure to change.

In America, Poles would, whenever possible, get permission to begin their own parishes, with Polish priests and Polish customs. By the late 1800s, more than 200 Polish American parishes had been established. Only ten years later, there were more Polish Catholics practicing their faith than any other Catholic ethnic group. Despite this, the Catholic Church restricted the creation of new Polish Catholic parishes and ordered that the existing parishes stop teaching the Polish language and culture in the parish schools. In 1897, a number of Polish congregations left the Catholic Church and established the Polish National Catholic Church (PNCC). This denomination still exists in the United States today and has parishes in Brazil, Canada, and Poland.

## Pope John Paul II

Many Polish Americans were overwhelmed with joy when Cardinal Karol Wojtyla (karol VOY-tee-yah) became Pope John Paul II in 1978. He was born in 1920 in Wadowice (VAHD-oh-viss), near Kraców. He grew up under the shadow of the Nazis and studied to be a priest in secret. During the war and after, he was a part of the underground movement that resisted the Nazis and then the Soviets. He made papal visits to Poland in 1979, 1983, and 1987 to show that the church was free and unafraid, even in the face of Communism.

When the pope visited the United States in 1979, the Polish American community turned out in full force, greeting him with Polish songs. People in Chicago, some wearing traditional Polish dress, waited for more than thirteen hours to see the pope's motorcade go by. A half million people came out to see him in Chicago's Grant Park. This was just the first of many visits by the pope to North America.

While the Catholic Church is still a big part of Polish American life, its authority over the family has lessened. However, people still attend services and volunteer to work in the parish, and many parents send their children to parish schools. Even those who have moved away from the church make it a point to participate in Easter and Christmas services.

Because of Poland's long history with Germany, some Polish Americans are members of the Lutheran faith, the Protestant sect that was founded by the German reformer Martin Luther in the sixteenth century. Although the church service in Lutheran churches has similarities to the Catholic mass, Lutheran clergy can marry and the congregation has a more democratic role in how churches are run.

Many Polish Jews came to America in the first half of the twentieth century to escape religious persecution. In America, they found the freedom to worship as they pleased. (To learn more about Judaism, see pages 31–32 in *The Newest Americans,* R–V.)

## Holidays and Festivals

The first Polish immigrants to America brought with them rich Easter and Christmas traditions. In America today, many Polish Americans, even if not religious, still follow these traditions.

On Christmas Eve, Wigilia (VI-gil-ee-a) is observed. The word Wigilia comes from a Latin word that means "to watch." And that's just what children of Polish descent do. They watch the skies at twilight to see who can spy the first star. Then the family sits down to a traditional Christmas feast. Under the table-cloth are a few pieces of straw to remind everyone of Christ's humble birth in a stable. An empty chair is at the table, ready for any hungry stranger who might show up at the last moment.

In America, Christmas Eve has become a time of family gathering and reconciliation. It's also considered a magical night in Polish tradition—animals are said to talk in a human voice and people have the power to tell the future.

In Chicago, many Polish heritage clubs sponsor Wigilia banquets. Customs that would be observed in homes in Poland have been transformed into American public events.

Easter is also celebrated with many customs. Eggs are dyed on Good Friday. In some homes, elaborately decorated hard-boiled eggs are prepared. These are called *pisanki*

(PEE-san-kee) or, if carved, *skrobanki* (skrow-BON-kee). The eggs are painted with patterns in wax and then dipped in dyes. The wax keeps the dyes from staining where the wax has been painted. Some eggs have designs of animals and flowers incised into their shells after they are dyed.

On Easter Sunday, Polish American families have their Easter baskets blessed by the parish priest. Although the baskets used to be like picnic baskets containing all kinds of foods, in America the baskets contain just the traditional American Easter goodies—decorated hard-boiled eggs and candy.

*Participants in the Pulaski Day Parade wear traditional Polish outfits and wave to the crowds that line New York City's streets for the annual event.*

# The Arts

*Popular singer Pat Benatar performs at the Wiltern Theater in Los Angeles. Benatar is of Polish ancestry.*

Although the polka is a dance of Czech origin, it became popular in Europe in the 1800s and made its way to Poland. In America, people of Polish descent play polka music at weddings, parades, and festivals. In the South, it has a country twang; in the North, the polka has picked up electric guitars and even a blues sound. Most polka bands have an accordion, drums, and a trumpet. Others add saxophone, guitar, and banjo. Set in two-fourths time, polka music is lively and fun.

Many Polish Americans have had an influence on the American symphony. The piano playing of Arthur Rubinstein (1887–1982) made him world famous. He played the music of the classical Polish composer, Frédéric Chopin. Rubinstein developed many symphony orchestras in America, such as the Cleveland Orchestra in Ohio.

In popular music, Polish Americans, like Pat Benatar and Huey Lewis, have also made their mark. Jazz drummer Gene Krupa (KROOP-ah) has influenced generations of jazz musicians.

Isaac Bashevis (bah-SHAY-viz) Singer has achieved world recognition for his literature. Singer's novels show the life of Polish Jews before World War II and the life of immigrant Polish Jews in New York after the war. He won the Nobel Prize for Literature in 1978.

Many Polish filmmakers fled to the United States in the 1980s to escape the repression of the Soviets. Director Agnieszka (ahg-NESH-kah) Holland is one of these political refugees. Her father was killed during an interrogation by the Polish secret police. Her parents' resistance to Communism meant that Holland was denied permission to attend film school in Poland. Instead, she studied film in Prague, Czechoslovakia. She has become well known for her movies

*Angry Harvest* and *Europa, Europa,* which she made in Poland and Czechoslovakia. *Angry Harvest* was banned in Poland in 1985. *Europa, Europa,* made in 1991, won the Golden Globe for Best Foreign Film. In the United States, Holland worked with Warner Brothers Studio, a studio founded by other Polish Americans, on a film version of the classic children's book, *The Secret Garden*.

## Food

Polish Americans love visiting. Entertaining guests with conversation, laughter, and food is an essential part of life. According to an old Polish saying, "When a guest enters the home, God enters the home."

Polish food ranges from elegant crepes to hearty stews. The variety of foods reflects the French, Swedish, German, Ukrainian, Jewish, and Italian influences in Poland's long history. With spices such as juniper, allspice, caraway, marjoram, and dill, however, Polish food has its own unique flavor.

Soups are a staple of the Polish American menu. Vegetable-barley, beet, creamed cabbage, pumpkin, and mushroom soup are just a few of the favorites. Chilled soups are made from fruits, like blueberries or gooseberries. Soup recipes are considered guidelines only, and cooking an unusual soup using leftovers is seen as a creative endeavor.

*Julia Balik has been making pierogie for more than 70 years. She works alongside other women of Polish and Eastern European ancestry at the Perfect Pierogie shop in McKees Rocks, Pennsylvania.*

Polish dishes often appear at American picnics and fairs. Kielbasa (keel-BAHS-ah), a spicy Polish sausage, is popular by itself or in casseroles. Potato salads, three-bean salads, cauliflower and celery-root salads have become staples at American get-togethers. Pierogi (peer-OH-gee), a puffed dough filled with a variety of meats, vegetables, or fruits, can be found at many ethnic fairs.

## Potato Pancakes

2 pounds raw peeled potatoes

2 eggs

3 tablespoons flour

salt

pepper

vegetable oil

sour cream

sugar

Grate the potatoes and place in a colander to drain. In a large bowl, mix the eggs and flour, stirring well. Add the drained potatoes and mix well. Add salt and pepper to taste.

Pour oil in a skillet until it is about 1/2-inch deep. Heat the oil over medium-high heat. To determine whether the oil is hot enough, carefully put a small drop of batter in the skillet. If it sizzles, the oil is ready.

Use a tablespoon to drop a pancake-sized ball of batter into the heated oil. Fill the pan with several pancakes. Flatten the batter with a spatula, making sure the pancakes are covered with the hot oil. Fry one side until brown and then flip and fry the other side until crispy. Place on a paper towel to blot excess oil. Serve the pancakes with sour cream or a sprinkle of sugar.

*Source: The Culinary Arts Institute's* Polish Cookbook

# CHAPTER SIX

Puerto
Ricans

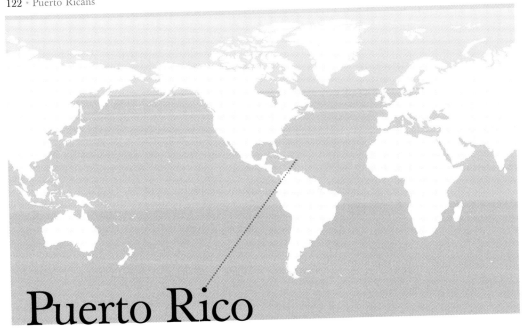

# Puerto Rico

is located southeast of Florida in the Caribbean Sea. The densely populated island of Puerto Rico is the easternmost and smallest island of the Greater Antilles chain. Puerto Rico is a commonwealth of the United States, which means that it governs itself under the supervision of the United States. All foreign policy and military decisions are made by the United States. The commonwealth includes several smaller islands— Vieques, Culebra, Culebrita, Palomino, Mona, and Monito— as well as Puerto Rico.

## A Quick Look Back

The first inhabitants of Puerto Rico settled on the coast between 5,000 and 20,000 years ago. Amerindians from South America migrated to the islands between 5 B.C. and A.D. 27. By the beginning of the tenth century, the Taino Indians, the ancestors of the people who would greet Columbus and his crew 500 years later, had a well-established agricultural civilization.

## A Spanish Colony

Christopher Columbus landed on Puerto Rico during his second voyage to the Americas in 1493. The Taino Indians showed him gold nuggets in the river and told him to take all he wanted. With that one act of kindness, the Taino guaranteed their own extinction. Spain began colonizing the island in the early 1500s, enslaving the Taino. By 1514, the brutal conditions suffered by the Taino diminished the population from 70,000 to 4,000. When the Spaniards' native slave labor source was depleted, they turned to Africa for more slaves.

As Puerto Ricans began to develop a strong national and cultural identity in the mid-1800s, they sought freedom from Spanish rule. In 1868, Dr. Ramon Emeterio Betances (ay-muh-TAY-ree-oh bay-TAHN-suhs) led a revolt against Spain, taking control of the town of Lares and declaring Puerto Rico an independent republic. The call for Puerto Ricans to arm themselves and fight against the Spanish government became known as El Grito de Lares (the Battle Cry of Lares). In 1897, Puerto Rico was granted autonomy. The grant of autonomy by Spain guaranteed Puerto Rico the right of self-government; approval of governors nominated by Spain; a *parliament* with checks and balances; as well as the rights to elect its own legislators, create its own currency, negotiate foreign treaties, and levy its own tariffs. Although welcome, Puerto Ricans' new autonomy was short-lived.

> **Did you know?**
>
> The Taino called their island Boriquén (bor-ee-KAYN), "Land of the Valiant People." The Taino were known as Boriqueños (bor-ee-KAY-nyohs), a name that many Puerto Ricans claim for themselves today.

## U.S. Rule

Spain became involved in revolutionary wars in Cuba and the Philippines at the end of the nineteenth century. When a U.S. warship that had been sent to Cuba to protect American citizens exploded and sank in Havana Harbor, the United States blamed Spain. Two months later, the United States declared war against Spain. This brief war, known as the Spanish-American War, lasted only a few months.

The United States used the fact that Puerto Rico was a Spanish colony as an excuse to invade the island in July 1898, a few weeks before the Spanish-American War ended. The United States had long been interested in Puerto Rico because it would provide a strategic military location, commercial potential, tourism possibilities, and natural resources. By October 1898, less than a year after Puerto Rico was granted autonomy by Spain, the United States was in control of the island.

# Legislation Affecting Puerto Rico

Gradually, Puerto Ricans were able to reap some of the benefits of becoming a possession of the United States. Under the Foraker Act of 1900, U.S. military rule ended and duty-free trade was established.

Puerto Rico was allowed to have an elected representative, called a resident commissioner, in Washington, D.C. At first, the resident commissioner had the right only to address federal departments. In 1902, the commissioner was granted the right to be present in the U.S. House of Representatives; the right to speak in front of Congress came in 1904. The resident commissioner continues to have only a voice, not a vote, in Congress.

*Thousands of Puerto Rican celebrants wave American flags during a rally celebrating U.S. citizenship at the Capitol in San Juan, Puerto Rico, in March 2000. President Woodrow Wilson granted Puerto Ricans citizenship in 1917.*

The Jones Act of 1917 granted Puerto Ricans U.S. citizenship, but they still have not been given the right to vote for the U.S. president. In 1952, Puerto Rico was granted commonwealth status, which gives Puerto Ricans more rights than if they remained a territory, but not as many rights as they would have with statehood. Puerto Rico wrote a new *constitution,* which was approved by the United States in 1952.

As a result of early legislation concerning Puerto Rico, the relationship between Puerto Rico and the United States is complicated. Puerto Rican men are eligible for the military draft and tens of thousands of them have died fighting in the U.S. military, but Puerto Ricans cannot vote in presidential elections. Residents of Puerto Rico do not pay federal income tax, but they are eligible for U.S. welfare benefits and food stamps. Puerto Ricans are American citizens, but the island does not have a voting member in Congress. Although overturning past legislation is not impossible, it has not been a priority for the U.S. Congress.

## Statehood, Commonwealth, or Independence?

Almost all Puerto Rican citizens are dissatisfied with their current relationship with the United States. Some citizens would like Puerto Rico to remain a commonwealth, but with more benefits from the United States and more freedom from U.S. control.

A number of Puerto Ricans, most of them from the upper and middle classes, want their island to become the fifty-first state of the United States. The process for becoming a state is long and complicated. A majority of the citizens of Puerto Rico would have to vote for statehood in a referendum. Then Puerto Rico could take the results to Congress and petition to become a state. This process is guaranteed under the First Amendment of the Constitution, which gives U.S. citizens the right to petition. A vote would be required in Congress before Puerto Rico could be granted statehood. If Puerto Rico became a state, citizens on the island would be given the right to vote for president and elect representatives to Congress. They would also have to pay federal income taxes.

A small number of Puerto Ricans staunchly support independence from the United States. They argue that self-government would allow Puerto Rico to preserve its cultural and linguistic identity, stimulate the economy, and strengthen democracy.

> **Did you know?**
>
> Over 80 percent of Puerto Ricans voted in the 1996 general elections on the island. Puerto Rico has one of the highest records of voter participation in election processes in the world.

# Puerto Rico Today

*Marchers protest U.S. test-bombing on Vieques island in Esperanza, Vieques, Puerto Rico, in October 2000.*

The densely populated island of Puerto Rico depends heavily on federal aid from the U.S. government for economic stability. Agriculture and manufacturing industries have adapted to the changing *economy* on the island. Important industries include pharmaceuticals, electronics, and textiles. Livestock and dairy production now provide more agricultural income than crops. Tourism and construction are the fastest growing industries on the island. Statistically, Puerto Rico has one of the strongest economies in the Caribbean, but over half of the island's residents still receive public assistance from the United States. Today, education is a high priority for Puerto Rico, as is evident in the island's overall literacy rate of 90 percent and its budget for education, approximately 40 percent of the government's budget.

## The Vieques Debate

The U.S. Navy presence in Vieques, a small island to the east of Puerto Rico, provides fuel to the fire in the debate over Puerto Rico's status. Many see the navy's treatment of the island as another reason that the current relationship between the United States and Puerto Rico is unsatisfactory. The navy annexed, or took over, more than two-thirds of the island in 1941 to use as a training area. The navy was drawn to the island by its availability, remote location, and sparse population. However, the island is far from deserted. The citizens of Vieques have been deeply affected by the navy's presence.

About 70 percent of the island of Vieques has been used by the U.S. Navy as a training area for target practice with live ammunition and war games.

Puerto Ricans worry about the noise, harm to the environment, and the health of the people of Vieques. Many on the island blame the high cancer rate (26 percent over Puerto Rico's average) on the navy's pollution. Although the United States has offered multi-million-dollar economic development packages addressing health and environmental concerns in return for the navy's remaining in Vieques, many Puerto Ricans believe that the ecological and environmental damage far outweigh any economic advantage.

New York
Pennsylvania
Connecticut
New Jersey
Florida
Puerto Rico

# Coming to America

I n the 1950s and 1960s, Puerto Rico had a predominantly agricultural economy, with high unemployment rates. The government wanted to diversify the country by adding industry, but feared that thousands of farm-workers would join those who were out of work. The U.S. and Puerto Rican governments encouraged agricultural workers to migrate to the United States in order to create a predominantly industrial economy in Puerto Rico. Many of the Puerto Rican immigrants settled in New York City. The United States provided economic incentives to U.S. companies that relocated factories and plants to Puerto Rico. This industrialization plan was called Operation Bootstrap. As a result of the assistance to create jobs and the mass migration of Puerto Ricans to the United States, Puerto Rico briefly gained economic strength.

Puerto Rico's economy was soon based on the export of manufactured products. Many of the jobs that were created were filled by women; the number of unemployed males remained high. Eventually, many of the U.S. companies moved their operations to countries with cheaper labor costs. Finally, in 1963, Puerto Rico passed the Industrial Incentives

| Puerto Rican Population in the U.S. | |
|---|---|
| New York | 1,068,364 |
| Florida | 450,677 |
| New Jersey | 378,696 |
| Connecticut | 214,838 |
| Pennsylvania | 204,492 |

Source: U.S. Census, 2000

Act to encourage companies to move their operations to Puerto Rico. Pharmaceutical and petrochemical makers were attracted to the island, where regulations were less stringent. The tourism industry in Puerto Rico has also grown. Today, the number of Puerto Ricans entering New York is largely offset by those returning to Puerto Rico. The circular migration of Puerto Ricans is based on economic opportunities. When the economy on the island is strong, many return to the island. When the economy on the mainland is stronger, they come to the mainland.

As Puerto Ricans settled in the United States, they formed supportive communities. They opened bodegas (Puerto Rican grocery stores), restaurants, and social and recreational associations in their neighborhoods. These neighborhoods helped keep communication open among Puerto Ricans in the United States and with Puerto Ricans on the island. Puerto Ricans in the United States often collaborated with other Latino groups to promote common social causes.

## What's in a Name?

In the United States, "Nuyorican" is a word used to describe Puerto Ricans who were born in New York City. The label is now most often associated with Puerto Rican artists. The Nuyorican Poets Café in New York City has become a stage where Nuyorican artists can express their creativity.

## *Spotlight on*
### JUAN "CHI CHI" RODRIGUEZ

Born in Rio Piedras, Puerto Rico, in 1935, Rodriguez began working as a golf caddy when he was six years old. He practiced his golf skills by hitting balls made from tin cans with a branch of a guava tree. By the age of twelve, Rodriguez's talent on the golf course was apparent.

Some say that Puerto Rican golf was born with Chi Chi Rodriguez. With his flamboyant personality and skill, he came to prominence as one of the top ten in the professional golf circuit in the 1960s. He won his last Professional Golfer's Association (PGA) tournament in 1979 and joined the Senior PGA Tour in 1985. Over the course of his career, Rodriguez won eight PGA tournaments and twenty-two Senior PGA tournaments. His lifetime earnings total over $7 million.

# Life in America

*Surrounded by her family, Marilus Pagan holds a picture of her grandparents, Angel and Gloria Pagan, who immigrated to Camden, New Jersey, in 1945. The Pagans were among the first Puerto Rican immigrants to settle in Camden, where one-third of the citizens claim Puerto Rican ancestry.*

Puerto Ricans were granted U.S. citizenship in 1917. Citizenship gives them the ability to move freely between Puerto Rico and the United States, but they still encounter some of the same obstacles as noncitizen immigrants. A strong Puerto Rican cultural identity fosters community and support among Puerto Rican immigrants.

Before Puerto Rico was granted commonwealth status, the United States forced schools on the island to teach only in English. After Puerto Rico became a commonwealth, Spanish was chosen as the official language on the island. The schools now teach in Spanish, but students also learn English. Few Puerto Rican immigrants arrive on the mainland without knowing any English.

## Family

A large percentage of Puerto Rican families on the island and the mainland are headed by women. Because women historically earn less than men, this has led to a large number of Puerto Rican families living in poverty.

Puerto Ricans have one of the highest poverty rates of any minority group in the United States. There are federally funded programs intended to assist families in poverty. Although many Puerto Ricans qualify for these programs, many hesitate to take advantage of them. Puerto Rican men have grown up learning that it is their job to provide for their families. When they are unable to make ends meet due to low-paying jobs, public assistance is a painful last resort. Puerto Rican women are also a proud group, but they are more willing to accept public assistance. They see it as a more logical choice than working for low wages and no benefits while paying high child-care fees to strangers taking care of their children.

In the United States, many Puerto Ricans live in extended families as a way to alleviate financial problems. Many households consist of several families living together. A child might share an apartment with brothers, sisters, parents, grandparents, nieces, nephews, aunts, uncles, or cousins. Although the living conditions may not be comfortable, the children are usually surrounded with love and strong family values.

Puerto Ricans value family above all else. The teen pregnancy rate among Puerto Ricans in the United States is one of the highest in the nation. Although the families of the pregnant teenagers may first be embarrassed and disappointed about the pregnancy, the strong bond among family members leads them to support and raise the babies of their teenage daughters.

## Work

### Did you know?

Puerto Rico has its own Olympic team and competes in the Miss Universe pageant as an independent nation.

Early Puerto Rican immigrants came to work on farms picking fruit or harvesting tobacco. Some found blue-collar work in factories. As the farms and factories became more technologically advanced, many of these workers were displaced. The job market now requires at least a high school education and high-level skills for most jobs. Many Puerto Ricans, especially women, find low-paying food service and cleaning jobs. Puerto Ricans who grow up on the mainland sometimes have better luck because education is more accessible in the United States. Because so many young people in poverty-stricken families have had to work, higher education is often not an option or must be delayed.

# School

As Spanish-speaking U.S. citizens, Puerto Ricans faced a language barrier when they *immigrated* to the mainland. To meet this challenge, the Puerto Rican community became a major player in the bilingual education movement. A lawsuit was brought against the New York City Board of Education in 1972 to obtain equal access to education for Puerto Rican children. As a result of the lawsuit, New York City began offering transitional bilingual programs in the 1970s to meet the needs of children who fell into the limited English proficiency category.

The U.S. Supreme Court ruled in 1974 that states must establish bilingual programs for children whose native tongue was not English. Over the years, this ruling has had far-reaching effects for many other non-English-speaking groups across the country. All children in the United States have the right to a free "appropriate" public education, which means that instruction must be suitably modified to assist each child's learning. Because some citizens are not aware of this right, they are silent while their children do not receive the education they are entitled to.

# Religion

The majority of Puerto Rican immigrants are members of the Roman Catholic faith. The next largest religion among Puerto Ricans is Pentecostalism, a Protestant Christian religion. Both of these religions, as well as other Protestant religions, have addressed the needs of Puerto Rican church members in America by offering a number of religious services in Spanish. Roman Catholic churches traditionally offer many programs to help the immigrants and newcomers in the congregation. The Pentecostal churches not only provide needed services to the poor and needy; they also work with members of the community to eradicate drugs and gangs from Puerto Rican neighborhoods.

# Holidays and Festivals

Puerto Ricans in the United States celebrate a number of religious holidays, but the Christmas season is one of the favorite times of the year. The festivities begin in early December and continue into January. Everyone looks forward to *parrandas, Nochebuena, Navidad,* and *Día de Reyes.*

One favorite activity is the *parranda* (also called an *asalto* or *trulla*)—a surprise caroling party. Small groups of carolers gather at the home of a friend, usually late at night when the friend is asleep. They begin singing *aguinaldos*—traditional Puerto Rican Christmas songs—and playing guitars and other instruments. The person who has been awakened must invite the carolers into the home for a party. After an hour or so, the hosts and the carolers move on to the next house. The *parranda* often lasts all night long, ending at dawn when the last hosts serve the traditional *asopao de pollo* chicken soup. In America, the festivities are usually shorter and carolers may stay at one house rather than move from house to house.

Nochebuena (Christmas Eve) is a time for family gatherings and parties. Traditional foods such as arroz con *gandules* (rice with pigeon peas), *pasteles* (meat-filled pastries), and *lechón asao* (roast pig) are often the centerpiece of Christmas Eve feasts. Midnight mass is an important part of Nochebuena for many Puerto Ricans.

On Navidad (Christmas Day) families honor the birth of Christ. Traditionally, Navidad is a day of quiet reflection and rest after the excitement of Nochebuena. However, most Puerto Rican families today have adopted the American traditions of Christmas trees and Santa Claus.

*A parade complete with large statues of the three wise men, or three kings, winds through East Harlem, New York, in celebration of the Christian holiday of Epiphany.*

Children eagerly anticipate *Dia de Reyes* (Three Kings' Day, or Epiphany), the January 6 holiday honoring the three kings who brought gifts to the Baby Jesus. On January 5, children fill shoe boxes with grass they have cut for the kings' camels. These boxes are placed under the children's beds before they go to sleep. During the night, the kings fill the boxes with gifts and candies. Three Kings' Day celebrations include great feasts and gatherings of family and friends. In America, many Puerto Rican children wait for presents from the Magi instead of Santa, although many second- and third-generation mainlanders now place more emphasis on Santa.

A lesser known festival, the fiesta of Santiago (Saint James the Apostle), is celebrated on July 25 with special Catholic masses, processions, street entertainers, and dancing. Because this date also marks the day Puerto Rico became a commonwealth of the United States, it is an occasion for political protest by some on the island.

Puerto Ricans in New York City celebrate their culture and heritage in June with the National Puerto Rican Day Parade. In 2002, over 100,000 people participated in the parade, which featured floats, singing, dancing, and marching. The celebration drew an estimated 3 million spectators.

## The Arts

The rich cultural heritage of the Puerto Rican people transfers easily into the arts. Even when Puerto Rican contributions are blended with other Latino contributions, the Puerto Rican input is apparent.

## Music

Puerto Ricans developed a music known as *salsa,* a mix of African American jazz and Latin rhythms. The music includes heavy use of percussion instruments and a lead singer using call and response. Salsa music has become very popular, even among non-Latinos. A number of Puerto Rican singers, including Ricky Martin, Marc Anthony, and Jennifer Lopez, have gained popularity in America in recent years.

## *Spotlight on*
### JOSÉ MONSERRATE FELICIANO

Acclaimed by critics worldwide as the "greatest living guitarist," José Monserrate Feliciano was born blind in Lares, Puerto Rico, on September 10, 1945. His family immigrated to New York City when he was five. At age six, Feliciano learned to play a concertina by listening to records. (A concertina is a small hexagon-shaped instrument that resembles an accordion, but with button-like keys.) Then he taught himself to play guitar.

Feliciano released his first album in 1964. In 1968, he crossed over to record in English, at a time when few Puerto Rican artists dared such a move. He has earned over forty gold and platinum records and six Grammy Awards. His most famous songs are "Que Sera," "Chico and the Man," and "California Dreamin'." His song "Feliz Navidad" has become a popular addition to the American Christmas music scene. East Harlem High School in New York City was renamed José Feliciano Performing Arts School in his honor.

## *Spotlight on*
### RITA MORENO

Rita Moreno was born in Humacao in 1931. She and her mother moved to the United States when she was five. Her mother hoped to find work and escape poverty in the United States. Moreno's father and brother were left behind in Puerto Rico; she never saw them again.

Though it was a drastic change from her life as the child of farmworkers, Moreno thrived in New York City, where her talents were quickly discovered. She was cast in Robert Wise's *West Side Story,* the famous 1961 film about Puerto Ricans in New York. When Moreno won an Oscar for her supporting role as Anita, she donated the money to the University of Puerto Rico for an acting scholarship.

In the 1970s, Moreno appeared on the children's television shows *Sesame Street* and *The Electric Company.* She hoped these appearances would provide inspiration to Latino children. "I am Latin and know what it is to feel alone and ignored because you are different," she said at the time. "My presence can tell a lot of children and some adults, 'Yes, we do exist, we have value.'"

Moreno made history when she became the first person to win all four of the biggest awards in show business: the Oscar (movies), Emmy (television), Grammy (music recording), and Tony (Broadway theater). She also became one of the few Latinas of her time to cross over into the American mainstream and gain international fame.

*Rita Moreno sings and dances in the 1961 movie* West Side Story.

## Art

As minorities, Puerto Ricans have often been overlooked in historical accounts of artistic development in America, even though they have made significant contributions to the art world. Poster art and printmaking gained popularity in Puerto Rico in the 1940s. Today, artists such as Lorenzo Homar, Myrna Báez, and Nayda Collazo-Llorens continue that tradition. Rafael Ferrer is one of the best-known contemporary Puerto Rican artists in America. His work ranges from oil paintings to sculpture to installments of avant-garde environments. The Taller Boricua (Puerto Rican Workshop), a gallery and studio in Spanish Harlem, cultivates the artistic creativity of youth in the New York City area.

# Food

Puerto Rican food includes ingredients from the various peoples that have inhabited the island. From the Taino come cassava and corn. The Spanish contributed chickpeas, cilantro, eggplant, onions, garlic, and coconut. The African slave trade brought green pigeon peas, which have become the national bean, plantains, yams, and okra.

Over the years, low-fat versions of some traditional dishes have become more popular, but for the most part, Puerto Ricans eat the same types of foods as their ancestors. As more varieties of fruits and vegetables that are native to Puerto Rico are grown in the United States, ingredients for traditional dishes become more affordable and easier to find for Puerto Rican immigrants.

## Arroz con Dulce (Puerto Rican Rice Pudding)

3 cups water

1 teaspoon salt

2 cinnamon sticks

6 whole cloves

1 1-inch piece fresh ginger, peeled and sliced

1 14-ounce can coconut milk

1 cup water

1 cup short-grain rice

1/3 cup dried currants or raisins

4 tablespoons shredded sweetened coconut

1/2 cup sugar

Ground cinnamon for garnish

In a large saucepan, combine the 3 cups water, salt, cinnamon sticks, cloves, and ginger. Bring to a boil. Pour the liquid through a colander into a bowl; discard the spices.

Combine the spiced water with the coconut milk and 1 cup water in a large saucepan. Bring the liquid to a boil. Add all the remaining ingredients except the cinnamon. Reduce the heat, cover, and simmer for 20 minutes. Remove the lid from the pan, stir, and cook for 15 more minutes, or until the rice is cooked. (All the liquid should be absorbed.) Pour onto a platter and sprinkle with cinnamon.

Serves 6 to 8.

*Source: Adapted from*
A Taste of Puerto Rico *by Yvonne Ortiz*

# Glossary

**civilization** a highly developed society that demonstrates progress in the arts and sciences, keeps some form of written records, and creates political and social organizations

**colony** an area or country under the control of another country

**Communism** a system of government in which the state plans and controls the economy and a single, often authoritarian party holds power, claiming to make progress toward a higher social order in which all goods are equally shared by the people

**Communist** a person who supports Communism

**conqueror** a person who gains control of a country by force

**constitution** a written paper that tells people what a country's laws are and how they will be governed

**coup** shortened version of coup d'état. Refers to the overthrow of a government, usually by a small group

**culture** the customs, beliefs, arts, and languages that make up a way of life for a group of people

**democracy** a government whose policies and leaders are directed by the people of the country

**descendant** a person whose ancestry can be traced to a particular country or ethnic group

**dictator** a leader who rules a country through force, often imprisoning or killing those who speak out against the government

**discrimination** the practice of treating people differently because of race or other characteristic

**dissident** one who is outspoken in expressing political disagreements with a government

**economy** how a country makes and spends money. In a strong economy, many people have jobs and can buy what they need. In a weak economy, people are often out of work and worry about whether they will be able to pay their bills.

**emigrate** to leave one country to live in another

**ethnic group** a group that shares the same language and customs

**exile** having to live in another country because of political or religious reasons; a person who is forced to leave his or her country

**guerrillas** people who work in small groups to attack their enemies, usually the government

**immigrant** a person who moves from one country to live in another

**immigrate** to come to a country with plans to live there

**parish** a district made up of neighborhoods presided over by a particular church and priest or bishop

**parliament** a legislative body made up of representatives

**quota system** a system of determining how many immigrants can enter a country each year; in this system, a foreign country or region is assigned a quota, or maximum number of immigrants

**refugee** a person who seeks safety in another country due to fears of imprisonment, torture, or death because of race, religion, nationality, or political beliefs. In the United States, refugee status is granted to those who apply for resettlement in the United States while they are still in another country.

**regime** a particular style of government; often used to describe a government that controls its people through force or oppression

**sanctions** punishments, usually economic, that one country or group of countries imposes on another, such as not letting that country buy or sell certain types of goods

**terrorist** individual or group that uses violence to intimidate or influence others, especially for political reasons

# Bibliography

American Muslim Alliance. "Mr. Saghir Tahir: Candidate for the New Hampshire House of Representatives," 4/2/01 http://www.amaweb.org/candidates/saghir_tahir.htm

Arellano, Amber, ed. "Beyond Cinco de Mayo: Latino Holidays and Cultural Customs." *National Association of Hispanic Journalists* http://www.nahj.org/resourceguide/chapter_4.html

Atkin, S. Beth. *Voices from the Fields.* Boston: Little, Brown, 1993.

Basra, Khalid Manzoor. "Music in Pakistan– The Story of Five Decades," 4/2001 http://www.the-south-asian.com/April2001/Pakistan%20music.htm

BBC. "The Mughal Empire." *Islam UK* http://www.bbc.co.uk/religion/religions/islam/history/mughal/index.shtml

BBC News. "Bianca Jagger Heads AIDS Campaign," 5/14/01 http://news.bbc.co.uk/1/hi/entertainment/showbiz/1330181.stm

——. *Country Profiles: Nicaragua* http://news.bbc.co.uk/1/hi/world/americas/country_profiles/1225218.stm

Borland, Katherine. "Folklife of Miami's Nicaraguan Communities." Historical Museum of Southern Florida http://www.historical-museum.org/folklife/folknica.htm

Bracero Justice Project http://www.bracerojustice.com/main.htm

Bradley, John. *Eastern Europe.* New York: Franklin Watts, 1992.

Brimner, Larry Dane. *A Migrant Family.* Minneapolis: Lerner Publications, 1992.

Bukowczyk, John. *And My Children Did Not Know Me: A History of the Polish Americans.* Bloomington: Indiana University Press, 1987.

Canabal, Maria E. *Poverty Among Puerto Ricans in the United States: JSRI Working Paper #32.* Julian Samora Research Institute, Michigan State University, East Lansing, Michigan, 1997.

Chorzempa, Rosemary A. *Polish Roots.* Baltimore: Genealogical Publishing, 1993.

Citizenship and Immigration Canada. "Eating the Nicaraguan Way." *Cultural Profiles Project* http://cwr.utoronto.ca/cultural/english/nicaragua/eating.html

Courtney, David. "Basic Overview of the Tabla." *The Tabla Sit* http://www.chandrakantha.com/tablasite/articles/overview.htm

Culinary Arts Institute. *Polish Cookbook.* Chicago: Consolidated Book Publishers, 1976.

Darling, Anita. "A Nation Tempered by Poetry." *Los Angeles Times,* 7/26/99 http://www.dariana.com/LATimes-2.html#anchor81854

Davis, Ann. "Fear Lingers in Pakistani Areas of New York City." *Wall Street Journal,* 11/13/02 http://www.sfgate.com/cgi-bin/article.cgi?file=/news/archive/2002/11/13/financial1058EST0057.DTL

Domowitz, Susan. "Pakistani-Americans Talk to Pakistanis about Muslim Life in the U.S." *U.S. Department of State International Information Programs,* 11/19/01 http://usinfo.state.gov/usa/islam/a111901.htm

Ferriss, Susan. "In Setback to Chiapas Peace, Zapatistas Reject Indian Law." *Cox Newspapers,* 5/01/01 http://www.coxnews.com/washingtonbureau/staff/ferriss/05-01-01COXMEXICO INDIANLAW0501.html

——. "Zapatista Rebels Arrive in Mexico City to Make History." *Cox Newspapers,* 3/12/01 http://www.coxnews.com/washingtonbureau/staff/ferriss/03-12-01COXMEXICO ZAPATISTAS03121ST.html

Garvin, Glenn. "Nicaraguans in U.S. Urged to Seize Amnesty." *Miami Herald,* 3/2/00 http://www.rose-hulman.edu/~delacova/nicaragua/amnesty.htm

González, Carolina, ed. "Where Are We From? Briefings on the Diversity of the Americas." *National Association of Hispanic Journalists* http://www.nahj.org/resourceguide/chapter_3.html

Graber, Karen Hursh. "Wrap It Up: A Guide to Mexican Street Tacos." *Mexico Connect* http://www.mexconnect.com/mex_/recipes/puebla/kgtacos1.html

Hayward, Mark. "City Man Visits Native Pakistan to Defend U.S." *Union Leader and New Hampshire Sunday News* (Web edition), 12/10/01 http://www.theunionleader.com/articles_show.html?article=7277

Hoobler, Dorothy, and Thomas Hoobler. *The Mexican Family Album*. New York: Oxford University Press, 1994.

Indiana University-Purdue University Fort Wayne. "Bianca Jagger: The Power of One." *1999–2000 Omnibus Lecture Series* http://www.ipfw.edu/omnibus/19992000/jagger.htm

Johnston, Joyce. *Puerto Rico*. Minneapolis: Lerner Publications, 1994.

Juda, Fanny. "William Walker." *Museum of the City of San Francisco*. (Excerpted from *The Grizzly Bear* 21 (4) Whole No. 142: February 1919) http://www.sfmuseum.org/hist1/walker.html

Kaye, Tony. *Lech Walesa*. New York: Chelsea House, 1989.

Kelly, Eric P. *The Trumpeter of Krakow and Other Stories*. New York: Macmillan, 1928.

Kent, Deborah. *America the Beautiful: Puerto Rico*. Chicago: Children's Press, 1991.

Knab, Sophie Hodorowicz. *Polish Customs, Traditions, and Folklore*. New York: Hippocrene Books, 1993.

Konczal, Lisa. *Assimilating into Hispanic America: The Case of Nicaraguan Immigrant Adolescents* http://www.fiu.edu/~iei/index/lisa2.html

Kott, Jennifer. *Nicaragua*. New York: Marshall Cavendish, 1995.

Mazhar, Uzma. "Eid ul Fitr." *CrescentLife* http://www.crescentlife.com/spirituality/eid_ul_fitr.htm

Microsoft® Encarta® Online Encyclopedia 2003. "Nicaragua." http://encarta.msn.com

——. "Nigeria" http://encarta.msn.com

Miles, Nick. "Nicaragua Ex-Leader Faces Immunity Vote." *BBC News*, 9/10/02 http://news.bbc.co.uk/2/hi/americas/2249274.stm

Milivojevic, JoAnn. *Puerto Rico*. Minneapolis: Carolrhoda Books, 2000.

Miller, Carlos. "Indigenous People Wouldn't Let 'Day of the Dead' Die." *Arizona Republic* http://www.azcentral.com/ent/dead/history/

——. "Valley Family Takes Yearly Tradition Seriously." *Arizona Republic* http://www.azcentral.com/ent/dead/history/history2.html

Minaret of Freedom Institute. "Growing Up a Muslim in America." Minaret of Freedom High School Essay Contest Winner, 1999 www.minaret.org/fp99.html

Muckley, Robert L., Jann Huizenga, and Adela Martinez-Santiago. *Stories from Puerto Rico*. New York: McGraw-Hill, 1999.

Nagel, Rob, and Sharon Rose, eds. *Hispanic American Biography*. New York: UXL, 1995.

National Oceanic and Atmospheric Administration. "Mitch: The Deadliest Atlantic Hurricane Since 1780." 1/25/99 http://lwf.ncdc.noaa.gov/oa/reports/mitch/mitch.html

Nigeria-Arts.net. *Home of Nigerian Arts on the Internet* http://www.nigeria-arts.net/

Ochoa, George. *The New York Public Library Amazing Hispanic American History*. New York: John Wiley, 1998.

Ortiz, Yvonne. *A Taste of Puerto Rico*. New York: Dutton Books, 1994.

Parr, Danny. *Lowriders*. Philadelphia: Chelsea House, 2001.

Perez y Gonzalez, Maria E. *Puerto Ricans in the United States*. Westport, CT: Greenwood Press, 2000.

Periyakoil, Vyjeyanthi S., Jennifer C. Mendez, and Amna B. Buttar. *Health and Health Care for Pakistani American Elders* http://www.stanford.edu/group/ethnoger/pakistani.html

Perl, Lila. *Puerto Rico: Island between Two Worlds*. New York: Morrow, 1979.

Polish Genealogical Society of America. "Polish National Catholic Church." http://www.pgsa.org/pncc.htm

Presidency of the Republic of Mexico. "Día de la Raza." *México for Kids* http://www.elbalero.gob.mx/index_kids.html

Reilly, Mary Jo. *Mexico*. New York: Marshall Cavendish, 1996.

Rohde, David. "Pariahs of the City: 24 Hours in a Cab." *New York Times,* 5/4/97 http://query.nytimes.com/search/article-page. html?res=9407EEDC1730F937A35756C0A 961958260

Rumbaut, Rubén G., and Alejandro Portes, eds. *Ethnicities*. Berkeley: University of California Press, 2001.

Santiago, Esmeralda. *When I Was Puerto Rican*. New York: Addison Wesley, 1993.

Schreibman, Tamar. "Safia's Choice." *Working Woman Magazine,* 5/2001 http://www.workingwoman.com/may_2001/ wmoy_01.shtml

Sheehan, Sean. *Pakistan*. New York: Marshall Cavendish, 1996.

Si Se Puede! Cesar E. Chavez and His Legacy. "Cesar E. Chavez." *University of California at Los Angeles,* 1996 http://clnet.ucr.edu/research/chavez/bio/

Stanley, Dick. "Treasurer Intent on Educating Hispanics." *Austin-American Statesman,* 7/28/02.

Tannenbaum, Jeffrey A. "Franchisee Inspires Others to Buy Their Own Outlets." *Startup Journal: The Wall Street Journal Center for Entrepreneurs* http://www.startupjournal.com/franchising/ franchising/199905271727-tannenbaum.html

Tejano Music Awards. "Artist Biography: Selena Quintanilla-Perez" http://www.tejanomusicawards.com/ selena.html

United Farm Workers. "The Story of Cesar Chavez" http://www.ufw.org/cecstory.htm

United States Census Bureau http://www.census.gov

United States Department of the Treasury. "Treasurer Rosario Marin" http://www.ustreas.gov/offices/treasurer/ rosario-marin.html

Walker, Judy. "Festival for Departed Souls Begins with Food." *Arizona Republic* http://www.azcentral.com/ent/dead/food/

Wilgoren, Jodi. "A Nation Challenged: The Pakistani-Americans; Isolated Family Finds Support and Reasons to Worry in Illinois." *New York Times,* 10/1/01 http://query.nytimes.com/search/article-page. html?res=9B0CE2DA153DF932A35753C1 A9679C8B63

Williams, Mike. "Coffee Glut Drives Central American Farmers Deeper into Poverty." *Cox Newspapers,* 4/28/02 http://coxnews.com/cox/news//static/cwb/ previous/williams/042802CENTAM- COFFEEGLUT.html

World Golf Hall of Fame. *Lee Treviño* http://www.wgv.com/hof/mem_year.html

Wrobel, Paul. *Our Way: Family, Parish, and Neighborhood in a Polish American Community*. Notre Dame, IN: University of Notre Dame Press, 1979.

Wtulich, Josephine. *Writing Home: Immigrants in Brazil and the United States 1890–1891*. Boulder, CO: East European Monographs, 1986.

Yusufali, Jabeen. *Pakistan: An Islamic Treasure*. Minneapolis: Dillon Press, 1990.

Zachary, G. Pascal. "Living the Highlife." *In These Times,* 7/19/02 http://www.inthesetimes.com/issue/26/19/ culture2.shtml

# Index